TEACH US TO NUMBER OUR DAYS

D1511147

TEACH US TO NUMBER OUR DAYS

A LITURGICAL ADVENT CALENDAR

Barbara Dee Baumgarten

MOREHOUSE PUBLISHING
HARRISBURG, PENNSYLVANIA

Copyright © 1999 by Barbara Dee Baumgarten

Morehouse Publishing

P.O. Box 1321

Harrisburg, PA 17105

Morehouse Publishing is a division of The Morehouse Group.

All rights reserved. No part of this book may be reproduced or transmitted in any form or by any means, electronic or mechanical, including photocopying, recording, or by any information storage and retrieval system, without written permission from the publisher, with the exception that permission is hereby granted to persons who have purchased this book and wish to reproduce these pages to make Advent calendars, for worship, church school, or other nonprofit use.

Unless otherwise noted, the Scripture quotations are from the *New Revised Standard Version Bible*, copyright © 1989 by the Division of Christian Education of the National Council of the Churches of Christ in the U. S. A. Used by permission. All rights reserved.

The Scripture quotations from the *Revised Standard Version of the Bible* (RSV), copyright 1946, 1952 © 1971, 1973, are used by permission.

Additional Scripture quotations are from the *New King James Version* (NKJV), copyright © 1979, 1980 and 1982 by Thomas Nelson Publishers, Inc., Nashville, Tennessee.

Symbol 33 is the logo for *The Catholic Worker,* designed in 1935 and revised in 1985 by Ade Bethune. Used by permission.

The hymn "Phos Hilaron" and the canticles "Surge, Illuminare" and "The Magnificat" are from *The Book of Common Prayer* (1979) of the Episcopal Church, as adapted into inclusive language by the Community of St. Francis in its CSF *Office Book*, copyright © 1996, San Francisco, California. Used by permission.

The meditation attributed to St. Ambrose is from *Lesser Feasts and Fasts 1991*, copyright © 1991 by the Church Pension Fund of the Episcopal Church. Used by permission.

The Collect for the Third Sunday after Easter (Christmas Eve prayer) and the Collect for the Holy Innocents are from *A New Zealand Prayer Book*, He Karakia Mihinare Aotearoa, copyright © 1989 by the Church of the Province of New Zealand. Used by permission.

Printed in the United States of America

Cover design by Dana Jackson

Baumgarten, Barbara Dee Bennett, 1955–
   Teach us to number our days : a liturgical Advent calendar / Barbara Dee Baumgarten.
      p.   cm.
   Includes bibliographical references.
   ISBN 0-8192-1765-4 (pbk. : alk. paper)
   1. Advent.   2. Advent calendars.   3. Handicraft—Religious aspects—Christianity.   I. Title.
BV40.B385   1999
263'.912—dc21
                                                                        99-30559
                                                                              CIP

For Bill

CONTENTS

PREFACE

"The problem with the Advent calendar is that it rarely matches, in length, the Advent season. I challenge you to make a calendar to fit the actual days of Advent," ventured my husband eighteen years ago.

The year of that challenge, I developed the junk-mail version of a liturgical Advent calendar, and over the years, it became a household tradition. Visitors, intrigued by the calendar, invariably asked how to make it, and many urged me to put instructions in writing. This book is dedicated foremost to my husband Bill and to all the folks who inspired its origins.

I will give you thanks for what you have done.
—Psalm 52:9

Around five years ago, I began to contemplate creating a permanent calendar that reflected the variable length of Advent and the season's fixed dates. Barbara Brandeburg's "Calendar Wall Quilt" (Cabbage Rose, 1995) spurred a flash of insight that led to the design of a fabric form complementing the desired function. My teaching others how to make the fabric calendar stimulated consistent calls for something written. My gratitude goes to all the folks who pushed and challenged me to frame in images and words my enduring affair with the season of Advent. I hope the contents of this book satisfy the need and are easy to follow.

I am indebted and grateful to God, who has impelled and guided this journey; to St. Francis of Assisi, Martin Luther and the German Lutherans who pioneered many of the traditions of Advent; to Michael Morris, O.P., who taught me a sound approach to iconography (the study of religious symbols); to Dora Crouch and Anne Thille, whose expert and honest reading of my manuscript was invaluable; to my editor at Morehouse, Debra Farrington, whose enthusiasm kept me going and whose, along with Val Gitting's, keen editorial perception and Christine Finnegan's technical expertise perfected this book; to my son Bennett, who let me know when my drawings were "no good" for coloring or cutting out; and most of all, to my husband Bill, whose challenge, support and love knows no bounds!

Chapter 1

The Advent Calendar

"Mom, when will it be Christmas?"

"In a few weeks, son."

"Mom, how many days 'til Christmas?"

Sigh. "Oh, not too many. Twenty-something."

"Mother! When will it be Christmas?" persisted young Gerhard of Munich, Germany, tugging on his mother's sleeve.

Exasperated, Mrs. Lang took out a large piece of cardboard and drew twenty-four spaces to mark the days from December 1 to December 24. She added some decorations and placed a sweet in each of the twenty-four spaces. Each day, young Gerhard Lang removed one sweet to mark off the days before Christmas. The calendar successfully alleviated Gerhard's incessant questions while increasing his excitement and understanding of the passage of time. Each year thereafter, Mrs. Lang made Gerhard a new calendar. Family and friends were intrigued by the homemade calendar and imitated it in their homes. Thus was born the twenty-four-day Advent calendar now mass-produced in assorted formats, shapes, sizes and materials worldwide.

Humankind has, from "time immemorial," gazed at the heavens and marked time: days by sunrise and sunset, months by the lunar cycle, and years by the solar cycle. Whatever the culture, a lunar or solar calendar was developed to relate the days to months and the months to years. The task was formidable since a year is always more than twelve months but less than thirteen.

Again, from "time immemorial," religious observances were connected with the cycles of the moon and sun. Christianity set its calendar by adopting and transforming observances from both the Jewish lunar calendar and the pagan solar calendar. The result is a two-cycle liturgical calendar consisting of feasts and holy days. The first cycle depends on the solar calendar and the fixed date of December 25 for the feast of the Nativity; the second hinges on the lunar calendar and the movable date for Easter Day. The Christian church year, in place by the fifth century, is a bit untidy, but its synthesis of Jewish and pagan roots rings true and has endured through the ages. Surely, God has been with humanity since "time immemorial" and prepares the hearts of all people for celebrations of God's presence. When Jesus came, celebrations of God were illuminated by his life, not abolished.

"As for me and my household, we will serve the LORD."
—Joshua 24:15

The Christian year, determined by the Nativity and Paschal cycles, is as follows:

I. *Nativity*

A. Advent, a short season of preparation for the coming of Jesus, opens the liturgical year on the fourth Sunday before Christmas.

B. Christmas, which celebrates the humble birth of Jesus, begins on December 25 and lasts for twelve days.

C. Epiphany falls on January 6; its season ranges from four to nine Sundays, depending on the date of Easter Day. It celebrates the manifestation of God-with-us, including the arrival of the Magi, the baptism of Jesus and the Transfiguration (last Sunday after Epiphany).

II. *Pascha* (Passover; hence, the Easter Season)

A. Lent, a time of penitential preparation for baptism and new birth, opens on Ash Wednesday, forty days (minus the Sundays of Lent) before Easter.

B. Easter Day is the first Sunday after the full moon that occurs on or after March 21. Easter Day is never before March 22 or after April 25. The Easter season, celebrating the Resurrection and Ascension (forty days after Easter Day), lasts for fifty days.

C. Pentecost Day, which falls on the seventh Sunday after Easter, celebrates the coming of the Holy Spirit, enabling the disciples to boldly witness to the risen Christ. The long season of Pentecost, sometimes called ordinary time, begins on the first Sunday after Pentecost, Trinity Sunday, and lasts from twenty-three to twenty-seven Sundays. The concluding Sunday of the liturgical year leads directly into the First Sunday of Advent by recognizing the eternal and cosmic reign of Jesus (Christ the King Sunday).

A liturgical calendar, besides marking time, helps us to deepen our relationship with God by encouraging us to align our days with the life of Christ. This book focuses on the first season of the church year, the brief season of Advent, by developing a liturgical Advent calendar. Unlike the traditional twenty-four-day countdown calendar, this liturgically based Advent calendar follows the actual dates of the church's Advent season and its variation of days from year to year. Like nature's year, Advent presents its own challenge to tally its days, since the season varies from twenty-two to twenty-eight days, as shown in the tables on the next page.

The secular calendar too often displaces Advent. As early as Halloween, "Christmas" decorations, music and enticements to buy, buy, buy begin to mask the quiet holiness of vigilance. Caught up in consumerism, we miss the signs of the coming Christ. We walk by them, we stumble over them, we fall into them, and still we do not see or understand who we are in Christ.

Instead, we covet the enticing indulgences of commercialism. The Advent calendar teaches us to count our days so that we may gain a wise heart (Psalm 90:12).

The anticipation of Advent is a response to the gospel of Jesus Christ. The secularization of Christmas has made Advent into a cornucopia of choices and demands. It can be the most harried time of year. We are called by God to live integrated lives with God, humanity and creation. Advent counters the dis-integration of the false life with a pause—to see, hear and watch for the coming of Christ. We let go of anxiety, fears and anger and pursue trust, justice and dependence on God. Within the context of Advent, attention to the gospel can restore us to an integrated life. Through symbolizing the progression of days on the calendar; through listening to the Word; through praying and singing our yearning; through smelling the greens, fasting and helping the stranger, we prepare for Christ's Advent.

Sun.	Mon.	Tues.	Wed.	Thurs.	Fri.	Sat.
27	28	29	30	1	2	3
4	5	6	7	8	9	10
11	12	13	14	15	16	17
18	19	20	21	22	23	24

The dates for the longest possible Advent season, beginning on November 27.

Sun.	Mon.	Tues.	Wed.	Thurs.	Fri.	Sat.
3	4	5	6	7	8	9
10	11	12	13	14	15	16
17	18	19	20	21	22	23
24						

The dates for the shortest possible Advent season, beginning on December 3.

This book is offered as a way to enrich and focus your household observance of Advent. It begins with a historical overview of how the season developed that is followed by a biblical reckoning of Advent themes and persons. The middle section contains the details of Advent: the symbols, persons, traditions and events you may want to include on your calendar. Each symbol has an accompanying scripture verse, description and suggestion. Finally, the last section provides three models for making a personalized calendar to mark the days of Advent. Consider making the junk-mail version once or twice before attempting the felt or quilted version. The final chapter contains the actual symbols for copying, coloring and transferring onto your calendar. (*Note:* The first year you make one of the cloth versions, you may want to specify coloring the symbol for the day's activity. At Advent's close, the symbols will be ready to transfer.)

The book and resultant calendar can be used to facilitate daily prayer and ritual, as well as to contribute to Christian education about the symbols, traditions, personalities and beliefs central to the season of Advent. The origins and meaning of Advent and some Christmas customs are presented, many of which are already popular practices. Yet many of the living traditions inherent to Advent are obscure in meaning, and other practices may be unfamiliar altogether. Learning the meaning of what we do strengthens our experience of Advent and ultimately our relationships with God and one another.

Advent is meant to be a time of introspection and reawakening of our true selves; therefore, setting a daily rhythm for using the calendar is well worth the effort. Just as we consult our secular calendars in preparation for the coming day, opening the Advent calendar and reflecting on a symbol's meaning provides a foundation to live by daily. The daily practice will equip you in your service to Christ. Take the experience signified by the calendar to the lighting of the candle(s) on the Advent wreath. (An Advent wreath devotional is provided in chapter 4.) Prayers and/or conversation may reflect on how the symbolization of the day impacts its event and your faith. Sometimes the impact may be too subtle to notice. Practice awareness of its influence. The more aware you become, the more manifest the coming of Christ will be in your life.

The goal is to make consistent use of the calendar and the Advent wreath. Days will occur when you are lucky to get the calendar opened, much less enter into any type of ritual! Such is the way of contemporary life. Do not judge yourself when you neglect the calendar or wreath. Simply be aware of your omission and allow this awareness to encourage the following day's observance. A prayerful, disciplined observance of Advent prepares us for an abundant celebration of Christ's arrival. Blessed are we who live in homes rich with focused rituals that awaken, condition, and strengthen us to receive Christ and enjoy the fruits of the coming!

How to Choose the Symbols for Your Calendar

"Choose this day whom you will serve."
—Joshua 24:15

The liturgical Advent calendar is designed to enhance our expectation of Jesus with spiritual and material preparation by accommodating and simplifying the variety of happenings during Advent. It pulls together the household life: religious and secular, work and play, individual, familial and social. The dates and symbols can be adjusted with ease to accommodate the flux of days within the season of Advent and the fluctuation of our lives from year to year. Symbolized blocks are selected to remind us of significant dates, special occasions, and routine events.

To choose what symbols to use, gather your household calendars: daily planners, general calendars, school calendars, church calendars, and so on.

On a sheet of paper, list the dates of the current Advent season. First note the dates for the four Sundays; they take precedence. Then map out the remaining dates you want to symbolize: special church activities, for example, Advent lessons and carols or *Las Posadas*; family events, such as a birthday or anniversary; the day to get the tree; and the day to bake cookies. Thumb through the pages of chapters 4, 5 and 6 for ideas. Once you have assigned dates to the occasions important to Advent and your household, you should have a list that looks something like this:

Date	Observance
November 30	First Sunday of Advent and St. Andrew's Day*
December 1	
2	
3	Birthday
4	
5	
6	Nicholas' Day
7	Second Sunday of Advent
8	Mary's Day
9	Pet birthday
10	
11	Make cookie dough
12	Bake and decorate cookies
13	Mail gifts
14	Third Sunday of Advent
15	Fetch Christmas tree
16	
17	Fire department Christmas party
18	
19	
20	Decorate tree and Hanukkah
21	Fourth Sunday of Advent and *Las Posadas*
22	
23	
24	Christmas Eve

With an eye to the unassigned dates on your list, read chapters 3, 4, 5 and 6. Select persons to remember or activities to do, filling in the open dates until no free dates remain. As you do so, read about the symbols that apply

The calendar-making directions in chapter 9, section 7 (pp. 108–110), describe how to handle a date that urges two observances, such as when the First Sunday of Advent falls on the feast of St. Andrew.

to the dates selected above and jot a note about all of the current days of Advent, as well as their assigned symbol numbers. The symbol numbers may be found in the caption under each symbol in chapter 10, where all of the symbols in this book are listed (in their order of appearance) with a key and cross-reference.

Chapter 3 surveys the biblical foundation of the three themes of Advent (past, future and present comings of Christ) and the three key figures of Advent (Isaiah, Mary and John the Baptist). Special holy days and persons essential to Advent but lacking a fixed date are covered in chapter 4, including the four Sundays of Advent (already noted on your list) and easily overlooked figures, such as Joseph, who need an assigned date.

The saints and the Great 'O' antiphons comprise chapter 5. When liturgical calendars are combined, every date during Advent, except December 11 and 15, commemorates a saint. A calendar that is used as a "Saints of Advent" commemoration calendar is conceivable, but the purpose of this household calendar is to "sacramentalize" and sharpen our present habituated lives. Therefore, you will more than likely select only a few persons from chapter 5, beyond the principal Advent commemorations of Andrew, Nicholas, Mary, and the 'O' antiphons, for your calendar.

Chapter 6 contains the miscellany of the Christmas season as applied to Advent. Many symbols are offered to serve the variety of ways that folks observe Advent. Be selective and focused in making your choices. You may add something new or different next year.

On your dated list, note activities and traditions that are essential to your household and faith community, and then complement them with symbols to enhance your Advent vigilance. In sum, the process is one of working from known dates to assigning meaning to open dates. A completed list may be something like this (dates listed above are bold):

Date	Observance	Note inside flap or pocket	Symbol
November 30	**1 Advent**	First Sunday of Advent. What is Advent? Who was Andrew? Set up Advent calendar and make wreath.	21/P-1*
December 1	Fire	Stock the woodpile—what does fire symbolize?	72
2	Silence	Practice a day of silence.	87
3	**Birthday**	Help mom celebrate her birthday.	62
4	Isaiah	What is a prophet?	17
5	Lights	Hang outdoor lights. What do they symbolize?	76

6 Nicholas	Why hang stockings? Write Christmas list.	40/P-2
7 2 Advent	What is the theme of the Second Sunday of Advent?	22
8 Mary	Who was Mary, and why is she special?	18/P-3
9 Pet Birthday	Be kind to all living creatures. How are animals kin?	58
10 Angels	What is an angel?	27
11 Baking	Make cookie dough.	59
12 Decorating	Bake and decorate cookies.	60
13 Lucy	Enjoy a "Lucy breakfast" and **mail gifts**.	46/75
14 3 Advent	Why do we rejoice on the Third Sunday of Advent?	23
15 Christmas tree	Get the Christmas tree.	66
16 Joseph	Why is Joseph important?	29
17 Party	Attend Fire Department Christmas party at 5:30 P.M. Begin reciting 'O' antiphons with O Wisdom.	81/ P-4
18 O *Adonai*	What does *Adonai* mean? What is the Law?	8/P-5
19 Magi	What do the Magi symbolize? O Root of Jesse.	30/P-6
20 Christmas tree	Why decorate a tree? O Key of David.	67/P-7
Hanukkah	What is Hanukkah? Eat something fried.	26
21 4 Advent	Fourth Sunday of Advent, Thomas and O Dayspring. *Las Posadas* at 5 P.M.	24/P-8 48
22 O King of Nations	How is Jesus the King of Nations?	53/P-9
23 Cleaning house	Finish getting ready for Christmas! O Emmanuel.	68 P-10
24 Christmas Eve	Advent closes; Christmas liturgy at 9:00 P.M. Replace wreath candles with white candles.	55

Once your list is complete, proceed to the instructions for making the calendar, found in chapters 7, 8 and 9. (The above list corresponds to the sample junk-mail version pictured.)

The P symbols signify major fixed dates to be made permanent on the calendar.

A Few Suggestions

Always be
ready.
—1 Peter 3:15

Some of the days of Advent require advance preparation. For example, supplies to make the Advent wreath on the First Sunday of Advent should be gathered before that Sunday. This is an easy thing to overlook since the First Sunday is the Sunday after Thanksgiving. If you opt to provide surprises on the feast of St. Nicholas, December 6, the stockings or shoes need to be set out the night before. The feast of St. Lucy on December 13 involves a special breakfast. Shopping needs to be done before opening the calendar on the morning of the thirteenth, lest you are caught short, without treats for a "Lucy breakfast."

When you select your Advent calendar dates, note the dates on your household and daily planners as well. For example, the purchase of the Christmas tree can be an event that requires many hours and thus you may select a date on your daily calendar or planner that is completely open. Noting the date on multiple calendars helps keep it free for the activity.

Baking and decorating cookies can be an all-day event that requires shopping in advance. Baking cookies is a messy business. Scheduling the baking just before housecleaning, so that you'll know the mess is temporary, can cut down on the stress. This is one reason this calendar works: you can relax knowing that what needs to occur during Advent is scheduled and reserved in advance. In other words, the Advent calendar and the household calendar are coordinated to work together and eliminate the harried stress that is all too common during Advent.

The Colors of Advent

They shall use
gold, blue, purple,
and crimson
yarns.
—Exodus 28:5

No season is more colorful than Christmas. Although Advent is not Christmas, it contains colors distinct to its expectant and preparatory character.

Gold signifies the wealth of those who watch for Christ, the Sun of Righteousness and the King of kings.

Blue, especially ensign or ultramarine, signifies hopeful expectation. It symbolizes the "glorious impossible" of Christ fully human, and the vast expanse of God's love, resembling the sky and waters, spreads over the entire earth. The dominant color of Advent, blue is traditionally associated with the Virgin Mary, whose constancy of faith reveals the goodness of God.

Purple, the color of royalty and power, heralds the coming of the King of kings. Purple reminds us that repentance and suffering lead to recognition of and alignment with God.

Crimson signifies the creative power of God evidenced in the fire of divine love, the blood of the martyrs and the Holy Spirit.

Rose, the color at dawn, heralds the imminent arrival of the sun—and Son. It is used on the Third Sunday of Advent.

White indicates Christ the Light, who is pure and holy love and the source of life. It is the color of Christmas.

Green represents the hope of spring and immortality.

Chapter 2

A Historical Overview of Advent

Jesus was born in Bethlehem of Judah during the reign of Herod. The dates Herod governed (37 B.C.E.–4 C.E.) enable us to approximate the year of Jesus' birth, but we do not know the time of year or the actual date. To add to the mystery, we do not know for certain when or why the feast of Christmas was set by the church on December 25. Literature about the early church before the fourth century mentions little regarding the Christmas festivals. When these feasts are mentioned, their origins are not discussed, only the fact that the feasts are kept. Late fourth-century texts tell us that the birth of Jesus was celebrated as the Epiphany, on January 6, in the East and as Christmas, on December 25, in the West. Advent is not mentioned until much later, toward the end of the sixth century.

Joseph went to [Bethlehem to] be registered with Mary, to whom he was engaged and who was expecting a child.
—Luke 2:5

By the end of the fourth century, the Christian calendar was essentially as it is today. The church had yet to discern whether a prescribed preparation for the feast of the Nativity was in order and, if so, what its shape and tone would be. The Advent season that eventually evolved depended on the Christmas-Epiphany interval. So, to appreciate Advent, we need to explore the development of Christmas.

Clement of Alexandria, a Greek philosopher who converted to Christianity about 190, wrote and taught in defense of Christianity. From his writings we can surmise that as early as 150 the birth of Christ was celebrated on January 6 in both the East and the West. Early Christians dated key events in Jesus' life based on the Jewish calendar, nature's seasons, and a date that agreed somewhat with other dates from his life. Once the date of the crucifixion was determined and Jesus' age was estimated, January 6 was deemed a sensible birth date.

The Egyptians' epiphany of the rebirth of their sun god may also have had a role in the January date. Celebrations of the divine child, Horus, were held at the end of the twelfth night after the winter solstice. Christians may have appropriated this feast to commemorate the birth of the Son of God.[1]

Ancient cultures lived by the sun and moon. Annually, the winter solstice and the lengthening days that followed were cause for great celebration. Ancient existence was influenced by the sun, which dictated the time to work and the time to rest, but most importantly, provided vitality to crops. As a result, the sun was deified. The religious ceremonies that celebrated the sun god may have influenced when and how Christmas is celebrated in the West. How much of a role specific worship of a sun god played in establishing our Christmas is unknown, but the most prominent pagan religious practices in and around Rome, including the *Saturnalia*, Mithraism, and *Deus Sol Invictus*, no doubt influenced the terrain of our Christmas feast.

The Roman *Saturnalia* was a week-long celebration of wild joy, from December 17 to 24, to honor the Italian deity Saturnus, or Saturn, the god of agriculture and time. Some Christians held that Saturn was in reality a prototype of Adam or Noah. Legend has it that when Noah first sighted the mountaintops above the subsiding flood, he held a feast in honor of Adam. Noah's feast instituted the *Saturnalia*.[2] Celebrations included the greening of homes, candle lighting, singing and gift giving. Goodwill to all prevailed, with equality between the rich and the poor, and the courts closed so that no one could be convicted of crime. The slaves were freed for the week and, during the feasting, were allowed to speak their minds and eat their fill while served by their masters. The theme of goodwill to all and many of the festive customs observed today find their roots in this ancient festival.

Twelve days after the winter solstice and peak of *Saturnalia*, December 21, came the *Kalends* of January, the first day of the new solar year. The twelve days between these two Roman festivals may have originated the twelve days of Christmas (December 25–January 5).

Mithraism spread to Rome during the second century and prevailed until the fourth century when its rivals, *Deus Sol Invictus* and Christianity, became dominant. Mithra was the Persian sun god, born December 25, who reigned in the middle zone between heaven and hell. God of light and defender of truth, Mithra helped the faithful fight the powers of darkness, was assumed into heaven and was to watch over all the earth until his second coming. Mithra celebrations were private and solemn. Many of the rites of Mithraism are similar to Christian rites. Adherents, primarily from the military ranks, were initiated by a baptism, honored the seventh day as sun day, celebrated Mithra's birth on December 25, and believed in the existence of heaven and hell, immortality of the soul and the resurrection of the dead. However, during the feast of Mithra's birth, only the king feasted; the people sacrificed horses to assuage their invincible god: *Deo Soli Invicto Mithrae*, "to the god the sun, the invincible Mithras."[3]

Deus Sol Invictus was the sun god adopted by Emperor Lucius Domitius Aurelianus in 274 as the official deity of the Roman Empire. Aurelian organized the numerous gods of Rome, indigenous and imported, into one symbol and then proclaimed *Deus Sol Invictus,* the sun god, the sum of all the attributes and functions of the gods. The religion of *Deus Sol Invictus* was intended to have a universal appeal to the Romans since it was a synthesis of religions. It answered the general religious trend toward monotheism and created unity and stability for the state. Aurelian took on the title *Deus* to politically unify Rome under him with one god, *Deus Sol Invictus*, to protect the state. In the process of adapting from other religions the comprehensive system of *Deus Sol Invictus*, the holiday of *dies Natalis Invicti*, "the birthday of the Unconquerable Sun," was established on December 25. The reserved festival of Mithraism was easily overshadowed by the the joyful abandonment of the *Saturnalia* and the events honoring *Deus Sol Invictus*—a grand celebration of the victory of light over darkness because the Rising Sun reigned supreme, protecting the empire and ennobling the emperor.

The Roman emperors enjoyed their deification and attendant power until the reign of Emperor Constantine from 306 to 337. Constantine's reign was dubbed "the Sun Emperorship" because he took the cult of *Deus Sol Invictus* to its extreme, claiming to be the personification of *Deus Sol Invictus* on earth until his conversion around 323. At that time Constantine dissolved his relationship with the sun god in favor of the Christian God, who created the sun. Constantine had already shown favor to the Christians with the Edict of Milan in 313, when he legalized Christianity. Slowly, the Christians won him over, to the point that he renounced his own deification and consequently his absolute power. When the sun cult fell from imperial favor, the status of both Christianity and secular life changed in Rome.

One change was the transfer of the date of the feast of the Nativity of Jesus Christ from January 6 to December 25. Since the actual birthday of Jesus was unknown, the previous amalgamation of the many pagan gods into *Deus Sol Invictus* provided a short step for supplanting the birthday of the sun god, the *Natalis Invicti*, with the birthday of the Son of God, *Sol Iustitiae*. Between 354 and 360, the feast of the Nativity, Christmas Day, was established in the Christian calendar as December 25.

Tracing the origins of Christmas and Epiphany is difficult enough, but gaining knowledge about the origins of Advent is harder yet. Its beginnings are sketchy. The terms Adventus, Epiphania, and Natale are all expressions for "Incarnation," and they were used interchangeably by the early church to name the feast that commemorated the birth of Christ. Since the term Adventus ("coming, arrival") was originally applied to the feast of the Nativity, it is difficult to sort out when and how it began to be used to designate a period before Christmas.

Observances of Christmas and Epiphany, feasts of Incarnation and manifestation, created an anticipatory climate during their preceding weeks, especially since baptisms were performed during Epiphany (outside of Rome). The joyful anticipation in Rome of festivities at Christmas and the penitential preparation for Epiphany baptisms were joined to create the season of Advent.

Baptism, a rite of initiation, requires a period of preparation. Early records suggest a period of preparation for Epiphany was observed in a synod of Saragossa, Spain, as early as 380. December 17 to January 6 was a time for adults to prepare for holy baptism and subsequent membership in the church. Required of the adults was daily church attendance—with shoes on—and fasting; the period had a penitential tone. Since the birth and baptism of Christ were celebrated on Epiphany, a prepared adult would be spiritually reborn through baptism on this day.

The writings of Bishop Perpetuus of Tours (461–490) mention a forty-day fast before the Nativity that began on November 11, St. Martin's Day. Martin, a gentle man who became Bishop of Tours in 372, was the founder of monasticism in France. After his death, legends sprang up around his life, attributing many miracles to him. The anniversary of his death, November 11, 397, quickly developed into a day of festivity. When Perpetuus became Bishop of Tours in 461, he set about prescribing procedures for celebrations and fasting during the church year. For the time from the feast of St. Martin, November 11, to the feast of Epiphany, January 6, Perpetuus prescribed fasting and prayer and the period became known as "Martin's Lent."

On November 17, 567, the Council of Tours met in the basilica of St. Martin (built by Perpetuus). The Council bid members of the church to fast or eat lightly three days a week during November and daily in December until December 25. Just as Lent was a period of spiritual preparation for the joy of Easter, St. Martin's Fast was an analogous time to prepare for the joy of Christmas. Both Lents were seasons of preparation marked by repentance for one's sins and by fasting. In 581, the Council of Mâcon extended St. Martin's Fast to include all of Gaul, and during the following two centuries the practice spread to Germany and England. By the end of the eighth century, a penitential period of prayer and fasting before Christmas was observed throughout most of Europe.

Meanwhile, the evolution of Advent was quite different in Italy. Christmas was a time of high festivity with feasting, celebrating, and abundant drinking, owing to the pagan joy of the *Saturnalia* and *Deus Sol Invictus* being transformed to joy over Jesus' birth. The New Year's festival was transferred from its pagan festivities to a focus on the Parousia, the end of the world with the glorious return of Christ and the Last Judgment. Fasting was not observed in the south, where joyful celebrations included the preparations for Christmas, which began on Christmas Eve.

During the sixth century, Pope Gregory the Great (590–604) inaugurated a season of preparation for Christmas called Advent, composed prayers and responses, and preached from a series of readings appropriate to the season. One late November a great storm ravaged the Roman countryside and Gregory used the Gospel of Luke 21:25–33 to comfort the people. Since this sermon took place on the first Sunday of December and the gospel reading focused on Christ's second coming, it has been kept by the church to this day as the reading for the First Sunday of Advent.[4] In addition, Gregory preached a number of homilies urging the church to blend the boisterous celebrations of Christmas with the already popular affection for the expectant Virgin. These sermons and the French acceptance of the Roman liturgy began the centuries-long integration of the clash between the festive Roman observances and the penitential period practiced in the north.

The ninth century opened with the solemn practices of fasting and penitence from Spain and Gaul and the feasting and merrymaking of Italy struggling toward synthesis. Rome adopted the penitential character and fasting. In the north, the season was shortened to five weeks and the liturgical texts of Rome were used. As a result, the solemnity and seriousness of the north began to mellow and the indulgence of the south became more reserved.

Finally, to alleviate the confusion produced by clashing practices, eleventh-century Pope Gregory VII (1073–1085) decreed the observance of a season of Advent that was to last through the four Sundays before December 25, beginning on the Sunday nearest to the feast of St. Andrew (Symbol 34), November 30, and ending on December 24—making the Advent season as long as four complete weeks or as short as three weeks and one day, just as is observed today. He declared that Advent would consist of two themes: 1) waiting with joy for the birth of Jesus in Bethlehem and 2) preparing with reverence for the second coming of Christ at the end of time. The fusion of joy and penitence, of expectation and hope, of birth and judgment set the foundation for the fertile Advent season we have today.

By the end of the thirteenth century, the Advent season had developed a theology that incorporated the threefold coming of Christ: first, it recalled the coming of Jesus in the flesh at Christmas (Symbols 1–14); second, it anticipated Christ's return, or Second Advent, on the Day of Judgment (Symbol 15); and finally, it announced Christ's coming into our hearts daily to transform our lives into Christ's likeness (Symbol 16). The whole work of Christ was summed up in these short weeks of anticipation.

However, attitudes common at the close of the first millennium overwhelmed the paradoxical character of Advent and it became characterized as penitential, dwelling on the end of the world, judgment, anger, death, gloom, terror, horror, relics, purgatory, and indulgences. Advent during the Middle Ages became a mini-Lent. This spirit of penance is still found in some of the readings, but Advent today is also meant to be a joyful season.

Laxity and excess in the church led to a Reformation during the 1500s. Martin Luther and others challenged unbiblical practices and beliefs in the church. As a result, reform occurred within the church and denominations emerged. Advent observances ranged from mild to nonexistent. The Roman

Catholic Church reaffirmed a solemn but joyful waiting period of four weeks with serious yet eager preparations for the Lord. Other reformers, more radical than Luther, eliminated the liturgical calendar altogether, including celebrations of Easter and Christmas. Only Sunday worship was commemorated, and all Sundays were the same. Over time, the radical groups mellowed to allow observances of Christmas and Easter, but an Advent season vanished among most Protestant groups.

The liturgically oriented Protestant denominations, especially the Anglican (Episcopal) and Lutheran branches, have recently developed a new appreciation for the richness of past patterns of worship and have returned to some historical forms of worship. When interest in church history flowered, the roots of worship were rediscovered and recovered. The process is ongoing today as the misunderstood and eclipsed Advent season is finding new meaning among many denominations. Confusion still prevails among denominations about what to do with Advent. Some use it as an opportunity to begin the Christmas season early, while others hold to its penitential rigors, which almost negate the joyful anticipation of the coming of Christ. More and more denominations, however, are learning about and celebrating a joyful yet penitential Advent. Advent wreaths (Symbols 21–24) are prevalent in many churches anticipating the coming of Christ. A common lectionary is read, proclaiming our longing for God's grace in our lives, our waiting for the birth of Christ, and our anticipation of the return of Christ, the Victorious Judge. Annually, Christians are invited to reflect on the mystery of *Emmanuel*, "God-with-us," while praying *Maranatha!*, "Come, Lord Jesus!" The Christian year dawns across denominational lines with Advent's heralding of God's ever-new arrival of Christ—at Bethlehem, at the end of time and in our daily lives.

Chapter 3

Biblical Markings

The Old Testament is filled with longing: longing for God, for justice, for the eternal king. Israel, aware of her corruption, places her hope in God-with-us, the Messiah whose divine presence will conclusively vanquish evil. Advent appeals for salvation and the coming Messiah, echoing the Old Testament longing for God. The weeks of Advent recognize Hebrew ancestors whose hearts burned with messianic longing: Nahum, Habakkuk, Zephaniah, Haggai, Daniel and Esther. Advent becomes Christmas Eve with the recollection of Adam and Eve, the opening of human history and the primal longing for God-with-us (see Symbol 55).

The coming of God as Messiah, who was and is and is to come, defines Advent. The source for this threefold coming—the past Incarnation, the future coming in glory at the end of time, and the present daily visitation of Christ—is scripture. Because the daily visitation theme historically developed after the themes of Incarnation (see below) and Last Judgment (p. 21), it normally is listed as the third theme. The past Incarnation and future coming of Christ fold seamlessly into the present.

This is the season where we relive the story of Israel and its expectations.
—Raymond E. Brown

The Biblical Foundation of Advent Themes: Hope for Christ's Coming

The Past: Incarnation

Old Testament stories tell of God's promise to be with us and of God's marvelous activity that ushers in salvation for the whole world. Allusions to the incarnational coming of God swim throughout the Old Testament and are the source for a path of twelve messianic markings, a series of lessons and carols, and the lineage of God incarnate.

You show me the path of life. In your presence there is fulness of joy.
—Psalm 16:11

Messiah Markings

Tree of Life. Genesis begins at the center of the garden, where we encounter the Tree of Life or Paradise tree (Genesis 2:9). It is a symbol of

Symbol 1

Symbol 2

Symbol 3

Symbol 4

Symbol 5

Symbol 6

Symbol 7

God's life-giving presence and of the promise of immortality when we walk in God's presence. Though we lost our right to share in the fruits of the Tree of Life, our yoke of suffering and death is broken on a tree by Emmanuel, who leads us into eternal life (Revelation 2:7).

The Dove. A symbol of the Spirit of God, the dove returns to Noah bearing an olive branch to herald God's reconciliation and ever-abiding peace with us (Genesis 8).

Rainbow. God sets the bow in the clouds as a visible sign of the covenant between the Creator and creation. It is a sign of God's promise never again to curse the ground (Genesis 9).

Bread and Wine. Melchizedek, king of Salem and priest of God Most High, whose name means, "my king is justice," offers bread and wine as a covenantal meal, blessing the "God Most High, maker of heaven and earth," deliverer from our enemies (Genesis 14:17–20). From its beginning, the biblical story gives a profound sense of salvation history and of God's unremitting plans. The covenant promises are the basis of our relationship with God: God reveals God's presence so that we may know God and who we are— God's beloved.

Seed of Abraham. In spite of humanity's consistent rebellion, God reveals God's Self so that we may know God as intimately as children know their mother and father. The seed of Abraham (Genesis 15) is the root of the sprout from which salvation will flower at the ripening of time, when "all the nations of the earth [shall] gain blessing" (Genesis 22:18).

Three Visitors to Abraham and Sarah. God visits Abraham and Sarah to speak to them about the birth of a son (Genesis 18:1–15) whose offspring will be as "numerous as the stars of heaven and as the sand that is on the seashore" (Genesis 22:17).

Jacob's Ladder. Like the Tree and rainbow, Jacob's Ladder is a symbolic "bridge" linking God with humanity. Angels descend and ascend a ladder between heaven and earth, bearing the message from God that Israel will be the harbinger of salvation to all humankind. The ladder leads to the gate of heaven, where God's covenant of dynastic blessing is renewed with Jacob, descendant of Abraham and Sarah (Isaac and Rebekah's son) (Genesis 28).

Burning Bush. When Moses encounters God in the burning bush (Exodus 3), he is empowered to lead the enslaved Israelites to freedom through the waters of the Red Sea (Exodus 14). Moses recognized in the fiery bush God-with-us, disclosing God's regenerative light and victorious might against evil (see December 18, *O Adonai*).

Symbol 8

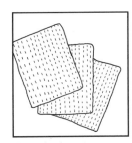

Symbol 9

Freedom. Matzah, the unleavened bread of slaves, is the bread the Jews made in haste for sustenance during their Exodus from slavery to freedom (Exodus 12). Matzah conveys the idea that freedom involves internal simplicity, not outward circumstances of status. The matzah, plain and flat, is not puffed up with pride and desires.

The Crown of David. The crown symbolizes divine rule and is the focus of messianic hope. An anointed shepherd (2 Samuel 5) proves to be Israel's greatest king, rising from humble status.

Symbol 10

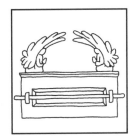

Symbol 11

Ark of the Covenant. Solomon, David's son, built the first Temple c. 960 B.C.E. to house the Ark of the Covenant, a symbol of God's presence. Jerusalem, the site of the Temple and God's dwelling place, becomes the center of the world (1 Kings 8).

Jonah and the Fish. The short book of Jonah admonishes against consistent refusal to trust God's presence and willful avoidance of God's call. God's redemptive love requires repentance and cooperation: forsake idolatry, give thanks to God, and practice compassion and justice toward all. Again and again we fail, yet God's promise is fulfilled. Jonah and the fish symbolize the full salvation accomplished by Jesus the Christ.

Symbol 12

Advent Lessons and Carols

In many churches, the First Sunday of Advent is observed with an Advent festival of lessons and carols, which usually takes place in the evening during a service of light. A typical service consists of a bidding prayer followed by nine Old Testament readings proclaimed alternately with hymns, canticles and anthems specific to Advent. Often this service marks the first lighting of the Advent wreath.

The lessons recount our creaturely status (Genesis 2:4–9, 15–25); our disobedience (Genesis 3:1–22), including the "proto-gospel" (v. 15), interpreted by many as the first hint that God will come and save our fallen race; God's response of comfort and promise of redemption (Isaiah 40:1–11, Jeremiah 31:31–34); our longing for God's presence (Isaiah 64:1–9); God's call to the prophet Isaiah (6:1–11); the prophetic revelation that God will come and save us (Isaiah 7:10–15, 11:1–9, 35:1–10; Baruch 4:36–5:9; Micah 5:2–4);

Hear the word of the LORD, O nations, and declare it in the coastlands far away.
—*Jeremiah 31:10*

Symbol 13

and our call to rejoice and sing because God promises a new heaven and a new earth (Isaiah 65:17–25, Zephaniah 3:14–18).

Hymns of longing and anticipation, such as "Sleepers, Wake!" and "Come, Thou Long Expected Jesus," echo the focus of the readings. Particularly appropriate is the Advent hymn, "O Come, O Come Emmanuel," drawn from the Great 'O' antiphons of Advent (December 17–23).

The Jesse Tree

In Isaiah, the Messiah's family tree is identified: the root of Jesse (Jesse was David's father). The house of David will produce an ideal king who will inaugurate the reign of peace, justice and universal knowledge of God.

In art, a reclining Jesse dreams of a genealogical tree that grows out of his loins with "leafs" in the tree that name the ancestors of Jesus. In homes and churches, a barren branch or bare evergreen is progressively laden with "leaves" of messianic lineage until the Jesse tree blooms on Christmas Day with the arrival of Jesus. The first "leaf" on the tree, Adam and Eve, represents the common origins of the whole human family. The Garden of Eden symbolizes the familial relationship of humanity and our rebelliousness that causes estrangement from God and one another.

A shoot shall come out from the stump of Jesse, and a branch shall grow out of his roots.
—Isaiah 11:1–2

Symbol 14

The New Testament opens with Matthew's genealogy, the model Jesse tree: "An account of the genealogy of Jesus the Messiah, the son of David, the son of Abraham." Verse 2 begins: "Abraham who was the father of Isaac" so that the story of Israel begets the story of Jesus Christ.[5] The lineage continues with Jacob, who generates the twelve tribes of Israel (two moons with twelve stars). Ruth (barley), Jesse's grandmother, is one of five women cited, all of whom have questionable marital status. She models that faithful perseverance, not birthright or status, is vital. Out of Jesse's humble home in Bethlehem, the young shepherd boy, David, is anointed king and his son Solomon exemplifies wisdom. After Hezekiah, the last of the faithful kings before the dispersion, the house of David falls into oblivion until Joseph agrees to wed Mary, the mother of God, and raise God's Son as his own. The son of Joseph is the long-awaited eternal king, the flower of Jesse's tree.

The Future: Parousia

The New Testament foretells the victorious return of Christ. The "day of the Son of Man" (Luke 17:24)[6] is Jesus' glorious Parousia. At a time indefinite, the "day of the Lord" comes to complete the work of salvation. Christ-with-us arrives in completion and eliminates all evil. It is the "day of judgment," when our behavior is assessed and we are called to account, finally and fully. On that day, Love-never-ending reveals who we are.

A symbol of the Last Judgment depicts Christ enthroned in majesty, surrounded by the four winged creatures of Ezekiel 1:10 and Revelation 4:6–7. Starting at Christ's right shoulder and moving counterclockwise, the creatures are a man, a lion, an ox and an eagle, symbolizing the four evangelists. As the winged man, Matthew, who opens with the genealogy of Jesus (Jesse tree above), stresses the Incarnation and the imminent kingdom. The winged lion represents Mark, whose gospel opens with the urgency of a lion's roar—"Prepare the way of the Lord!"—and closes with the Resurrection, also symbolized by a lion. The sacrificial ox present at the holy birth of Jesus, fully human and fully divine, is Luke's symbol, stressing the atoning death of Christ to save all humankind. John, the eagle, soars to the loftiest heights to affirm that Jesus is the incarnate Word of God (1:14).

The Present: Daily Visitation

Amos, a shepherd and prophet of social justice, proclaims God's hope for justice.

Our vocation is to watch for Jesus who *is* Lord, here and now. Love God by practicing justice and kindness daily. Our judgment hinges upon recognizing Christ, present in all people, especially the *anawim*[7]:

> Then the righteous will answer him, "Lord, when was it that we saw you hungry and gave you food, or thirsty and gave you something to drink? And when was it that we saw you a stranger and welcomed you, or naked and gave you clothing? And when was it that we saw you sick or in prison and visited you?" And the king will answer them, "Truly I tell you, just as you did it to one of the least of these who are members of my family, you did it to me." Matthew 25:37–40

Christ promises to be with us always, "I am with you always, to the end of the age" (Matthew 28:20). The entire corpus of the New Testament letters (Paul, Peter, James, Jude, and John) is written to believers to emphasize the active lordship of Jesus Christ. The letters bid us to remember the original message of Jesus' victory over death, to realize Christ present within the church. Like the apostles on the road to Emmaus (Luke 24:13–35), don't our hearts burn with the love of God when they are opened by Christ's presence?

Throughout scripture we are taught to watch for God-with-us, to repent for our disobedience and to rejoice in Christ's daily presence. Then we will

Beloved, we are God's children now; what we will be has not yet been revealed. What we do know is this: when he is revealed, we will be like him, for we will see him as he is.
—1 John 3:2

Symbol 15

But let justice roll down like waters, and righteousness like an everflowing stream.
—Amos 5:24

Symbol 16

be prepared to welcome the one who came humbly in the flesh and will come again in glory at the Last Day.

The Key Figures of Advent: Isaiah, Mary and John the Baptist

Our hopeful expectation of the coming of God's reign is nowhere more compelling than in the lives of the three biblical figures, Isaiah, Mary and John the Baptist, who incarnate the meaning of Advent. These three clearly exemplify Advent vigilance. Awake in God, they recognize God's arrival. In their acceptance of God's Advent, God comes for all of us: their vigilance facilitates God's Incarnation. The longing of Isaiah for the Messiah, the expectation of Mary, mother of God, and the recognition of the Christ by John the Baptist illuminate a threefold theology of Advent. (Note: Isaiah and John the Baptist do not have assigned dates during Advent. Honor them on an open date on your calendar. Mary is remembered on December 8.)

Longing: Isaiah

Eight centuries before the birth of Christ, when Israelite society was crumbling, Isaiah warned the people to repent and trust God to avoid impending destruction. After their ruin and exile, when life became extremely cruel and bleak, Isaiah comforted the Jews with assurances of God's love and promise. The prophetic voice of Isaiah proclaims the glory of the Most Holy God, the persistence of human sin, and God's immutable love.

Isaiah is the Advent prophet who warns, consoles, and bears hope. He refines the Old Testament longing for God into a hope for a messianic king who will usher in a new age when all creation will see God's glory: God will come to save us. Our eyes will be opened, our hearing unstopped, our speech filled with songs of joy (35:1–10). Prepare and watch for God-with-us, he cries. Traditionally, Isaiah is depicted holding a scroll foretelling the Incarnation: *Ecce virgo concepiet et parium filium.* The Latin phrase is the text:

> Therefore the Lord himself will give you a sign. Look, the young woman is with child and shall bear a son, and shall name him Emmanuel (7:14).

In his ninth chapter, Isaiah expresses longing for the ideal king who will restore the ravaged land to its former glory, who embodies the best qualities of Israel's heroes: the leadership of Moses[8], the courage of David, the wisdom

Then I heard the voice of the Lord saying, "Whom shall I send, and who will go for us?" And I said, "Here am I; send me!"
—Isaiah 6:8

of Solomon. The passage, commonly read on Christmas Day (since it is one of the clearest messianic passages in the Old Testament), promises that the Savior will be more than a human summation of Israel's great leaders, but will be a divine agent who incarnates God. In Jesus of Nazareth we recognize the Messiah who comes humbly in the flesh, who comes to overthrow evil and restore justice to all nations, who is active in our lives.

The latter sections of Isaiah, chapters 40–66 (Deutero-Isaiah or Second and Third Isaiah), are prophecies written some 150 years after Isaiah during the Babylonian exile (c. 539 B.C.E.). Within this corpus are four suffering servant songs,[9] incredibly incisive prophecies of Jesus' ministry. In these songs, we are given the character of the One to come, the One for whom we are to watch. The servant remains perfectly aligned with God even in the midst of overwhelming suffering. With gentle strength and patience, the servant brings God's word, the source of justice and loving compassion, to all nations. Yet the path of salvation is costly: it is paved with the suffering of the innocent servant. The servant, one with the people, intercedes through suffering to God for others, for us. The servant, one with God, remains uniquely innocent of sin so that to know the servant is to know God.

The suffering servant songs signal hope in spite of appearances. Rather than beholding the darkness that covers the land, we watch for the dawning of the everlasting light that reveals God's glory (60:1–3). Vigilant, we recognize the Messiah's coming. Courageous, we live as the servant community, identified with the *anawim*, the least of humanity, acknowledging the Messiah's daily advent. Expectant, we hope for Christ's return. Waiting with Isaiah, we sing the *"Surge, illuminare"*:[10]

> Arise, shine for your light has come, and the glory of God has dawned upon you. For behold, darkness covers the land; deep gloom enshrouds the peoples. But over you our God will rise, and the glory of the Most High will appear upon you. Nations will stream to your light, and rulers to the brightness of your dawning. Your gates will always be open; by day or night they will never be shut. They will call you, the City of God, the Zion of the Holy One of Israel.

Symbol 17. The six-pointed star, made from two interwoven equilateral triangles, represents the six days of creation, the shield of David and the seal of Solomon. The two triangles symbolize the meeting of God and humanity that was fulfilled in the Messiah. The vision of the redeeming light of the Messiah propels Isaiah's insistence that we prepare our soil to welcome the Messiah's coming. Therefore, this symbol for Isaiah is a tractor driven by the six-pointed star of David.

Violence will no more be heard in your land, ruin or destruction within your borders. You will call your walls, Salvation, and all your portals, Praise. The sun will no more be your light by day; by night you will not need the brightness of the moon. God will be your everlasting light and your glory.
—Isaiah 60:1–3, 11, 14, 18–19

Symbol 17

Then Mary said, "Here am I, the servant of the Lord; let it be with me according to your word."
—Luke 1:38

Symbol 18

Incarnating: Mary, the mother of God

Mary is the blossom of the shoot from the root of Jesse, the rose whose center is the site where God and humanity meet. A rose with its myriad petals emanating from a hidden center reminds us that all creation is connected to one center. The story of the Fall describes our wandering away from the center and our ensuing loss of life. Mary reverses the "sin of Eve" by calling us back to God.

A number of flowers represent Mary; the rose, symbol of manifestation and completion, is the Advent flower. Although a traditional title for Mary is *Rosa mystica*, the "mystical rose," the principal flower of Mary is the lily, symbolizing her purity and chastity. Legend has it that the lily sprouted from the tears Eve shed when she was evicted from the Garden of Eden. The lily is often shown in a vase, signifying that Mary is the vase, or vessel, of the Incarnation, the *Vas spiritualis*. When Song of Solomon 2:1 ("I am the rose of Sharon, a lily of the valleys") is attributed to Mary, the song bespeaks devotion to God; God, in turn, bestows upon her the grace to become the mother of God.

After Gabriel announces to Mary that she is favored by God and is to bear a son, who is Emmanuel (Luke 1:26 f., Matthew 1:18 f.), all creation awaits her response—the very Advent of Christ hangs on her willingness to accept the angelic message. All through the ages Mary's response echoes, "Here am I," your servant. And this is precisely the response Isaiah asked for from his people! And this is precisely the response God asks for from us daily.

God asks Mary to give her whole self over to God in spite of fear: fear of the angel, fear of God's announcement, fear of Joseph's reaction to her pregnancy, fear of her people's accusation of fornication. Fear, the incipient enemy of God, is transformed into trusting obedience through vigilance and expectation. When we, like Mary, are faithful people who are able to see Christ, fear gives way to love and devotion. Then with Mary we can sing: God's "mercy is for those who fear [God]" (Luke 1:50). Mary's acceptance of Gabriel's announcement is, in large part, due to her daily discipline of prayer, watchfulness and expectation of God's Advent.

Finally, Mary bids us to have a joyful expectation of God's arrival. Advent marks the final days of waiting and preparation before the imminent birth. We are all pregnant with God when we listen for and to the heartbeat of God's presence, when we open our selves to God's growth within us, when we nurture ourselves and one another with faith-filled hearts, when we rejoice in God's arrival and are obedient to God's urgings. We, with Mary, are called to be God-bearers, to carry Christ-with-us into a broken, oppressed and needy world. God arrives. Be awake, prepare, and join with Mary and the great chorus of Christians who sing through the centuries at the vesper light:

My soul proclaims the greatness of God,
    my spirit rejoices in God my Savior;
    for you have looked with favor on your lowly servant.
From this day all generations will call me blessed;
    for You, the Almighty, have done great things for me,
    and holy is your Name.
You have mercy on those who fear you in every generation.
You have shown the strength of your arm,
    you have scattered the proud in their conceit.
You have cast down the mighty from their thrones,
    and have lifted up the lowly.
You have filled the hungry with good things,
    and the rich you have sent away empty.
You have come to the help of your servant Israel,
    for you have remembered your promise of mercy,
The promise you made to our forebears,
    to Abraham, to Sarah and their seed forever.

The Magnificat—Luke 1:47–55[11]

Recognizing: John the Baptist

John the Baptist ceaselessly calls us to prepare for the new Exodus, to repent from our lives of sin and live lives of justice. He *is* the Advent watch person. With threats and ravings, he badgers us to face injustice, suffering and violence. John is clear and bold in his prophecy of Jesus' coming. To welcome the Messiah, we must repent and be healed. John informs us that following the Messiah, that being ready for Christ's Advent, requires repentance, changed behavior (cf. Luke 3:10–17) and courage. As bold as he is though, John readily gives way to the Christ: "he must increase, but I must decrease" (John 3:30); "I am unworthy to untie the thong of his sandals" (Mark 1:7, John 1:27). Like John, we are to expect and to point to another, to give way to Christ, who enters our lives.

John concludes the Old Testament messianic longing and initiates the New Testament recognition of the Messiah's Advent. He exemplifies self-denial and dutiful obedience even to death. John condemns our hiding behind religiosity. God is not interested in how "religious" we are; God calls us to lead authentic and just lives.

John is Jesus' cousin and complement. God's forgiveness and love are found in the meeting of John and Jesus. Together they weave the fabric of wholeness between God and humanity, between lover and beloved, between Creator and creation. The Christian calendar, following the gospel's testimony that

A voice cries out: "In the wilderness prepare the way of the Lord, make straight in the desert a highway for our God."
—Isaiah 40:3

Symbol 19

Mary conceived six months after Elizabeth (Luke 1:26–38), indicates the paradoxical yet complementary "yin-yang" nature of their relationship. The birth of John is celebrated on June 24, Midsummer Day, the apogee of long days of light, while the birth of Jesus is celebrated six months later, when the long night of darkness reigns. John's mother, Elizabeth, was old and in her barrenness had given up all hope of having a child; Jesus' mother, Mary, was a young virgin, ready to bear a child. John's father, Zacharias, was a priest of the Temple and his natural father; Jesus' father, Joseph, was a carpenter and a legal father (Symbol 29). John lives an ascetic and zealous life; Jesus lives a communal and gracious life. John baptizes with water for repentance; Jesus baptizes with the Holy Spirit and fire (Matthew 3:11). Shared is their identity with the *anawim*. John and Jesus uniquely and harmoniously call us to God through solidarity with the people of God.

Just as the pagan celebrations around the winter solstice were adapted to celebrate the birth of Jesus, so too were the pagan customs celebrating the summer solstice adapted to celebrate the birth of John the Baptist. Prominent in these celebrations is the use of light. The birth of Christ is celebrated, in the Northern Hemisphere, with fires in our hearths (Symbol 72); the birth of John the Baptist is celebrated with outdoor bonfires. The fires burn outside beckoning us to prepare for the coming of the one who burns within our hearts (Symbol 16). While the pagan feasts celebrate the reception of cosmic light to encourage its return for regeneration of their crops, Christians receive the light of Christ that guides our return to God for redemption. The summer bonfires, christened "St. John's fires," burn all night to welcome the dawn of the longest day of the year and to honor John, "a burning and shining lamp" (John 5:35). The fires remind us of our need to repent and burn away old faults in preparation for the yule fires, which burn all night to welcome the Christ, the Light of the world, into our homes and hearts.

Another complementary custom is the use of a wreath. During Advent, we use a wreath with four candles lit progressively week by week to herald the coming of Christ (Symbols 21–24). To celebrate the birth of John, a wreath filled with candles creates a symbolic indoor bonfire and reminds us of the summer solstice. The feast of John the Baptist celebrates the summer light that will fade away and reminds us to prepare for the true Light that comes at the darkest hour yet shines eternally.

Both birth festivals are connected with the solstice of the sun. Solstice means, "sun-stands-still" and suggests that the sun stands still in its arc farthest from the equator before commencing its return arc to the north or south. Because we move away from our center, we need to stand still, pause, turn around (repent) before we can begin our return journey to God. The births of John and Jesus bid us to stop, be still and know God (Psalm 46:10).

Symbol 19. John symbolically wears the blue tunic of love with the red mantle of sacrificial truth. He carries a long-stemmed cross, prophetic of the one for whom he prepares.

A Conclusion

In the closing book of the Bible, John the Divine gathers both Old and New Testament longings for the consummation of salvation by the One who was and is and is to come. The Bible closes with a prayer expressing our deepest Advent longing for Christ's coming:

Symbol 20

> "See, I am coming soon; my reward is with me, to repay according to everyone's work. I am the Alpha and the Omega, the first and the last, the beginning and the end." Blessed are those who wash their robes, so that they will have the right to the tree of life and may enter the city by the gates…. "It is I, Jesus, who sent my angel to you with this testimony for the churches. I am the root and the descendent of David, the bright morning star."
>
> The Spirit and the bride say,
> "Come."
> And let everyone who hears say,
> "Come."
> And let everyone who is thirsty
> come.
> Let anyone who wishes take the water of life as a gift….
> The one who testifies to these things says, "Surely I am coming soon."
> Amen. Come, Lord Jesus (Revelation 22:12–14, 16–17, 20).

Chapter 4

Changing Dates of Advent and Their Symbols

During Advent, we prepare for the "the glorious impossibles": the coming of God in the flesh as Messiah, in glory at the end of time, in our hearts daily. Intentional living is the only way we may hope to recognize God's arrival. Preparation with daily devotions, fasting and acts of kindness ready our minds and hearts to welcome God-with-us. Inner simplicity and silence help us to open ourselves to recognize Jesus the Christ. The Advent of Christ transfigures the world if we would only remove the blinders from our eyes and see. See Christ in the mundane, in the stranger, in the interruptions. So too, the Advent calendar is a tool that helps us to transform the blinding inundation of commercialism and materialism into a visual order that recognizes the holy in the array of images, in nature and in our traditions.

Advent progresses from the first square tagged, when a lone candle burns, to a compendium of twenty-two to twenty-eight days and a flame of four lights. This progression marks our movement from quiet attention to increased activity. Through it all, the focus of the season is sustained when we deliberately mark our days with an Advent calendar and our weeks with an Advent wreath. Central to the calendar are the four Sundays, the holy days and the biblical figures addressed in this and the following chapter. They map a way to observe a vigilant and holy Advent. Be alert! Jesus is coming soon!

> *The Glorious Impossibles are those things that bring joy to our hearts, hope to our lives, songs to our lips.*
> —Madeleine L'Engle

The Advent Wreath

The first Sunday of Advent is marked by setting out the Advent wreath in homes and churches. Week by week, the wreath announces the coming of the Light of the world. Its increasing light signals the approach of the true Light, who conquers darkness and the shadow of death.

Wreaths of greens or flowers intertwined into a circle have been used through the ages to honor royalty, victors, and the deceased. An evergreen wreath with candles is the quintessential Advent symbol. Its circle of evergreens represents everlasting life and its ring of flames represents eternal wisdom, divine illumination and the coming of the Messiah (see Symbol 28).

> *"I am the Alpha and the Omega," says the Lord God, who is and who was and who is to come, the Almighty.*
> —Revelation 1:8

The wreath, with four upright and equidistant candles, represents the four weeks of Advent. A candle is lit on the first Sunday during a short ritual. Each subsequent Sunday one more candle is lit, until all four are burning. The progressive lighting of the candles reminds us of the coming of the true Light at the darkest hour. The more candles that are lit, the closer the arrival of the Light of the world.

Candles on a wheel were lit by early agricultural communities in the hope of turning the wheel of the sun's orbit toward the earth once more. The wheel adorned with four candles became a Christian symbol when the Lutherans of east Germany made use of an Advent wreath in their homes as early as the sixteenth century. They adapted the light and fire theme to represent their hope for the coming light of life, Christ, into their midst. A focus for daily Advent devotions in the German Lutheran home, the wreath has moved into homes and church sanctuaries across denominational and geographic lines.

No universal tradition exists for the color and names of the four candles in the wreath. Traditionally, purple candles symbolize the penitential nature of Advent. Today, many use three blue candles, to highlight the expectant hope of Advent, and a rose candle, lit on the third Sunday, to punctuate the cause to rejoice—the true Light is coming soon! Some assign biblical personalities to the candles: Isaiah, John the Baptist, Mary and the shepherds. Others designate thematic names such as promise, light, love and hope. Here, we use watch, repent, rejoice, and recognize.

Making the Wreath

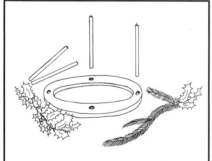

Make or purchase a circular form. Cut four equally spaced holes to fit standard taper candles. Attach evergreen branches (see Symbol 70) with wire or string until the form is covered. Position three blue- and one rose-colored candle on the wreath. Hang, situate on a table, or set where the Christmas tree will be placed. It should be obvious and accessible.

On the First Sunday of Advent and each evening during the week, light the blue candle directly across from the rose candle. On the second Sunday and during the week, light the first candle and moving clockwise, the blue one next to it. On the third Sunday and during the week, light the two blue candles and the rose candle. On the fourth Sunday and during the week, light all four candles.

On Christmas Eve, attach fresh evergreens and position a fifth, white candle in the wreath's center. Light this "Christ" candle during the twelve days of Christmas.

Advent Wreath Devotional

Set a regular time each day to light your Advent wreath and pray. Be disciplined: guard the time allotted for a daily devotion from distractions and lapses. When more than one person resides in the home, allow everyone in the household to have a part in the devotions. One person reads, another lights the candles, and another offers special prayers. Alternate who does what.

Opening: Recite the versicle and name the candle while it is lit.

Reader: The Redeemer shall come (Isaiah 59:20).
All: A Light to lighten a world in darkness (Luke 32:2).
Reader: The candle of watching (weeks 1–4).
repentance (weeks 2–4).
rejoicing (weeks 3–4).
recognizing (week 4).

Reading: Read the scripture and meditation that goes with the day's symbol on your Advent calendar, or tell what the symbol means in your own words.

You will do well to be attentive to this as to a lamp shining in a dark place, until the day dawns and the morning star rises in your hearts.
—2 Peter 1:19

Prayer: Say the following prayer, progressively adding the appointed phrase week by week, or if a saint is commemorated, say the appointed prayer that follows the meditation.

God our Light,
quiet our minds that we may watch for you (weeks 1–4);
    Expose our sins that we may repent and prepare for you (weeks 2–4);
    Reveal your love that we may rejoice in serving you (weeks 3–4);
    Open our eyes that we may recognize and welcome you (week 4); make our lamps shine and proclaim to the world that darkness is at end; there is Light for those who seek it and love for all. Amen! Come, Lord Jesus!

Silence and Intercessions: Offer any special prayers you may have.

Conclusion: You may conclude with the *"Phos Hilaron"* (p. 75), *"Surge, illuminare"* (p. 23), *"Benedictus"* (Luke 1:68–79) or another suitable Advent hymn. Beginning on December 17, conclude with "The Magnificat" (p. 25) and the appointed 'O' antiphon.

Closing versicle:

Reader: Jesus Christ is the Light of the world.
All: Come and save us, God of light!

The Four Sundays of Advent

First Sunday of Advent: Watch

Today is the First Sunday of Advent, the first day of the liturgical year, the church's New Year's Day. But we don't begin the season and year at the beginning. Instead, Advent opens with stirring readings about the last days. Just as Christ comes "like a thief in the night" (I Thessalonians 5:2), so Advent interrupts our busy, well-intentioned lives with a summons to "wake up," to put on the armor of light and watch for Christ.

The First Sunday of Advent foretells the last things in order to admonish us to tend to the first things. How we behave today, how we treat ourselves and others, matters ultimately. From Genesis to Revelation, we are taught the necessity of vigilance and right behavior *now*, in light of the Messiah's past Incarnation and future final Advent. The coming of Christ at the Last Judgment reveals that our judgment hinges upon how we treat Christ, present in all people, especially the least lovable, since *all* are members of Christ's family.

Watch as God watches us: with eyes of love and mercy. Be on guard against dissipation and complacency now, in light of God's coming. Keep on the lookout for Christ's activity in your life and in the world; remain awake to tend to the sick and brokenhearted through the night; mind the progression of weeks during Advent with discipline and prayer to make ready for the coming of Christ in humility, in glory, in us.

Second Sunday of Advent: Repent

John the Baptist compels us to make ready the way of the Lord. Confess the Christ who came humbly, a babe in a manger. Proclaim Jesus the Christ, who is the merciful and just one, the light of righteousness. Jesus comes among us and invites us to repent, to ask the light of righteousness to shine into our hearts so that we may become aware of our errant ways, confess them and be forgiven. As we look forward to vindication from evil, we must change our ways or we will live in total darkness. A terrible day is levied when we follow the illusion of darkness and try to bargain our way back to God through ritual and gifts. One way exists to heal our broken relationships, the way of light and truth and justice.

God sent a messenger, John the Baptist, to call us back to God so that we are prepared to recognize Christ. What opportunities have you had to see Christ, but instead have chosen not to see; to hear Christ, but instead have chosen not to hear; to minister with compassion, but instead have chosen to take offense at someone's unlovable qualities? As watchers for Jesus, we are

"And what I say to you I say to all: Keep awake."
—Mark 13:37

Symbol 21

"Repent, for the kingdom of heaven has come near."
—Matthew 3:2

Symbol 22

asked to examine our behavior: when we willfully chose to be blind, deaf, lame or in prison. Name an occasion when you refused to see Christ because you were locked into your own busyness and selfness. Repent. The two lit candles on the Advent wreath are visual aids: the first, the watch candle, prompts us to see, and the second, the candle of repentance, helps us to see more clearly. Let the growing light remind you to watch for opportunities to see, hear and love yourself and others. Let the light remind you to turn to God now and to prepare your heart for Jesus' arrival.

Third Sunday of Advent: Rejoice

Rejoice! It is Jesus who is coming soon, radiating unbridled love for us. He makes the blind see, the deaf hear, the lame walk; the lepers are cleansed, the dead receive life, the poor are blessed. And when we practice faith in our everyday actions, when we courageously follow Jesus, we too are blessed. The shape of our experience is transformed because we come to know intimately the compassionate love of Jesus. Our anxiety, fear and loneliness are changed to a new perspective of peace, hope and communion.

"Are you the one who is to come?"
—Matthew 11:3

Symbol 23

We light three candles: the first rouses us to watch for the light that comes quickly to vanish the darkness; the second summons us to repent and prepare for Christ; the third reassures us that we are loved and are healed by that love. Rejoice! Make ready for the God who passionately loves us by loving what God loves: mercy, kindness and justice. This love brings joy.

Prayer for others promotes the fullness of Christ's reign. Pray intentionally for people close by and far away, for those in the church and those who have no faith, for those who suffer, for those who are in trouble, and for those who have no one to pray for them. Pray for the most unlovable of all: those who have wronged you. Reach out to others across the miles, with different points of view and from the various social strata by praying for them. You will make a new place for Christ in your heart.

"The Lord is with you."
—Luke 1:28

Fourth Sunday of Advent: Recognize

The fourth candle is lit. The wreath shines forth with its full brightness to show that Jesus *is* the fulfillment of the Old Testament prophecies and longings for the Messiah. Jesus is *Adonai*, the "I am" revealed to Moses; Jesus is the suffering and triumphant servant of Isaiah; Jesus is wisdom, of the root of Jesse, the key of David, the Dayspring, the King of kings, Emmanuel. Our hearts leap with joy when we recognize the One who comes. And we are blessed because we have believed and have accepted the invitation to participate in the beloved community of God:

Symbol 24

The Word leaps down from heaven's portal;
Changed are we by such a babe:
Into Godness we are made.

The scriptures this week focus on Mary, the mother of God: the Annunciation to Joseph (Matthew 1:18–25), the Annunciation to Mary (Luke 1:26–38) and the visitation (Luke 1:39–49). We tend to picture the Annunciation as a clear moment of an angelic apparition—Mary had no doubt that the visitor was a messenger from God. But one may wonder and ask: would Mary have been able to recognize Gabriel if she had not been a person of prayer, piety, humility and expectation? Mary's faithful, daily attention to God prepared her to recognize the Annunciation, making it possible for her to be fully present for this history-shattering moment.

Through vigilance, repentance and prayer we have marked the days of Advent. We have readied ourselves to know with God-certainty those moments when Christ appears. This week pray, "God's will be done, not mine," and ask, "Am I grasping for or accepting my beloved status?" Depend on God and practice the presence of Christ so that when Jesus appears, you will be prepared to faithfully respond: "Let it be done unto me according to your word."

Special Days

Ember Days: Wednesday, Friday and Saturday of the Third Week of Advent
Conforming to the seasonal changes of the year, many ancient cultures observed rites of prayer and sacrifice that culminated in a seed or harvest festival. These nature festivals sought the favor of the gods to assure bounty. Instead of a celebratory event, though, the Hebrews observed four fasts of mourning to remember their destruction.[12] These fasts were calls to repent their sins of injustice and infidelity; to turn back to God; and to practice mercy, justice and faithfulness. The prophet Zechariah encouraged the fasting Jews to watch for the messianic age when all mourning would cease because God who is sovereign would fulfill God's promises for all people.

The early Christians combined the pagan seed and harvest festivals and the Jewish fasts of mourning into joyful fasts of gratitude for God's blessings. By the fourth century, three days (Wednesday, Friday and Saturday), called Ember Days, were appointed to precede the seasonal feasts of bounty. Since the apostles fasted and prayed before the laying on of hands (Acts 13:3, 14:23), Pope Gelasius, in 494, designated the Ember Saturdays as times for all members of the church to pray and fast for God's blessings and grace upon

Thus says the LORD of hosts: The fast of the fourth month, and the fast of the fifth, and the fast of the seventh, and the fast of the tenth, shall be seasons of joy and gladness, and cheerful festivals for the house of Judah: therefore love truth and peace.
—Zechariah 8:19

Symbol 25

those preparing for ordination. In 1085, Pope Gregory VII assigned Embertide to be on the Wednesday, Friday and Saturday of the Third Week of Advent, the First Week of Lent and the First Week of Pentecost and after Holy Cross Day, September 14.

Traditionally, the Ember Days of Advent are devoted to Mary and are occasions for prayers commending the fruits of human nature, children, and expectant women to God's blessings. The descent of the Holy Spirit symbolizes the priestly order of all believers by baptism and the bestowal of God's abundance on the faithful.

The third week of Advent is a time to fast and pray with marked intentions: fast for those who are hungry and suffer; fast and when hungry meditate on fears, appetites and attitudes that thwart your relationship with God; fast to prepare your body, mind, and soul for God. Pray for all ministers of the church, especially those about to be ordained; pray that God may guide your ministry; pray for those pregnant and those barren; pray for the children of the world, especially orphans. Engage in a work of mercy and justice; sing Psalm 148; welcome a stranger with alms, a meal and a warm bath.

Hanukkah

The Jewish feast of lights that usually falls within the Advent season recalls the victory of the Jews, led by Judas Maccabeus, over the Syrians in 165 B.C.E. The Jews had been subjected to a cruel and oppressive rule under the Syrian king Antiochus Epiphanes. He forbade the Jews to observe their religion, and he tried to force them to make sacrifices and to worship the Greek god Zeus. A Jewish priest, Mattathias, followed by his son, Judah Maccabee, organized a small band of Jews to revolt against the Syrian oppression. After three years of fighting, the Maccabees, as the Jewish band came to be known, triumphed and regained their freedom. The Jews' first order of business was to clean, purify and rededicate the Temple. The menorah, a seven-branched candelabrum symbolic of the seven days of creation, seven continents and seven planets, which had been darkened during the oppression, was relit. It was meant to burn perpetually, and great concern arose when only one day's supply of the special burning oil could be found. At the menorah lighting, joyful prayers of thanksgiving for freedom and for the oil were offered. By a miracle, the oil burned for eight days, the exact amount of time it takes to make the special oil!

Six days before the new moon of December, Hanukkah, or the festival of lights, is celebrated by the Jews for eight days to remember their religious freedom, their weakness made strong, and the miracle of light. The Hanukkah menorah, sometimes called "Chanukah" to distinguish it from the Temple menorah, is an even eight-branched candelabrum, with a ninth

Then Judas and his brothers and all the assembly of Israel determined that every year at that season the days of dedication of the altar should be observed with joy and gladness for eight days, beginning with the twenty-fifth day of the month of Chislev.
—I Maccabees 4:59

Symbol 26

branch—the "Shamash," or lighter candle—set apart. Just after dark on each night during Hanukkah, the candles on the menorah are lit successively until all eight candles are burning brightly on the final night. Households set the burning lights of freedom in a window to exhibit to passers-by: when all is dark and hope wanes, the light of the ever-faithful God shines bright and reigns victorious. After candle lighting and prayers, gifts are exchanged, foods fried in oil are enjoyed and dreidl is played.

On an evening during Hanukkah, honor the Jewish faith by reciting Psalm 30 during your Advent candle lighting; serve latkes, doughnuts or other fried food; and/or learn to play dreidl. (*Note*: Hanukkah begins at sundown the day before its calendar date; i.e., if Hanukkah begins on December 20, the first candle is lit at sunset on December 19.)

Biblical Figures

Are not all angels spirits in the divine service, sent to serve for the sake of those who are to inherit salvation?
—Hebrews 1:14

Symbol 27

The following biblical figures are prominent in the Christmas cycle but do not have assigned dates during Advent. They may be assigned an open date on your calendar.

Angels

Angels are our heroes and God's messengers: Michael slays the dragon of evil and leads us to peace; Raphael heals our infirmities and guides our journey on earth; Gabriel, the Advent angel, announces the coming of the Messiah. Angels convey to humanity God's enduring love and mercy. Unlike humanity, angels are purely spiritual beings that are portrayed youthful, androgynous and winged because they transcend time, gender and space. Like humanity, they have free will. Those who chose the way of God are the graced ones that guide us with benevolence to enlightenment; those who chose against God are the evil spirits led by Lucifer into exile and eternal damnation. To Daniel, Gabriel announces the end of the Babylonian exile and the coming of the messianic age (Daniel 9:1–27); to Zacharias, the impending birth of John the Baptist (Luke 1:13–20); to Mary, the paramount news of her being chosen in grace to bear the Christ child (Luke 1:26–38); and to the shepherds, the arrival of the Christ child (Luke 2:8–14). Recall a time when you suspected you were entertaining an angel. What was "angelic" about the visitor?

Symbol 27. An angel floating in space, with its right hand raised in benediction, is the herald angel who announces the birth of Christ; the trumpeting angel (Symbol B-2) announces the day of judgment.

Elijah

Elijah the Tishbite of Gilead was one of Israel's greatest prophets and is the Old Testament prototype of John the Baptist. He lived a solitary life in wilderness caves, and he warned Israel and her kings Ahab and Ahaziah (873–851 B.C.E.) to forsake their evil ways and turn back to the one true God, Yahweh. He averted death by ascending in a whirlwind into heaven in a chariot of fire (2 Kings 2:11). Elijah indicates that the Messiah will come when few love God, when darkness and great suffering prevail. Malachi names Elijah as the precursor of the "day of the Lord," and in the Dead Sea Scrolls he becomes the forerunner of the Messiah. Today, Jews leave an empty place at the Passover table in expectation of Elijah's return; Christians recognize the return of Elijah in John the Baptist. His symbol, a flaming wheel, is the biblical forerunner of the Advent wreath.

Lo, I will send you the prophet Elijah before the great and terrible day of the LORD comes.
—Malachi 4:5

Symbol 28

Joseph

God calls us to obedience, which means that we are called to align ourselves with God and God's way of justice and mercy. At its heart, obedience is following the way of Jesus taught in the Gospels. It is not a forced submission to something foreign to us but compliance with the Law written on our hearts. A hardened heart is impatient with God, doubting God's love and sovereignty. It negates God's way through pride and self-reliance particularly when things are not going "our way."

Joseph was a "just man" (Matthew 1:19), which means that he lived the Torah "blamelessly according to all the commandments and regulations of the Lord" (Luke 1:6). Things were certainly not going his way: his community was discontent with God's apparent absence; hope for the coming of the Messiah had faded; and his betrothed had obviously fornicated! Joseph was in a bind: how could he put Mary away (follow the Law) without shaming her? Joseph trusted God. He agreed to take Mary as his wife and to name the child, making himself the legal father. He fulfilled the Law and the prophets by giving Jesus continuity with the house of David. Joseph's cooperation "reconciles profound obedience to the Law with an acceptance of Jesus."[13] With Mary, Joseph realizes the depth of God's plan in the Law.

Yet, God did not pave a way of ease and success just because Joseph obeyed. Quite the contrary—little is known or said about Joseph He was a poor carpenter, a pious Jew of the house of David, an honorable husband and father who was sent into exile with his family. His dossier is simple: he was a righteous man. Joseph models the value of gentle humility and patient obedience in the everyday duties of life. We, too, are called to such a life.

Is not this the carpenter's son?
—Matthew 13:55

Symbol 29

They set out; and there, ahead of them, went the star that they had seen at its rising.
—Matthew 2:9

Symbol 30

There were shepherds living in the fields, keeping watch over their flock by night.
—Luke 2:8

Symbol 31

Magi

The Magi are an anonymous group of magicians and astronomers who follow a star to the Christ child. They, like us, are stargazers on a pilgrimage to find Jesus. Tradition in the West sets their number at three, whereas in the East it sets it at twelve. An audience with Herod and valuable gifts for the holy child evidence their wealth and royalty. Their gifts symbolize who they saw: the King of kings (gold), who is fully human (myrrh) and fully divine (frankincense). The kings, representative of all nations and peoples of the world, journey to pay homage to Jesus the Christ, Savior of all nations.

The Bible is often critical of magi, or magicians. They are enemies of God because they try to manipulate the supernatural for their benefit rather than follow the ways of God. Yet, God leads even the enemies and welcomes their gifts into the fullness of the kingdom.

Shepherds

Shepherds are common folk like you and me. They live ordinary lives and have ordinary jobs. The shepherds around Bethlehem were Jewish commoners—often despised—who did not let the banality of the everyday numb their task of watching through the night. Their vigilance allowed them to witness the glory of God, hear the good news of the Messiah's birth, and recognize the child in the manger. The humble shepherds contrast with the wealthy Magi. Together, they exemplify that Christ came for Jew and Gentile, slave and free, poor and rich: all are one in Christ Jesus.

Chapter 5

Fixed Observations during Advent and Their Symbols

"A saint is a sign of God," stated Thomas Merton. The life of the saint "affirms that Christ *lives*: that He is risen from the dead, that our faith therefore is not in vain,… and that in yet a little while Christ will come again to gather us to Himself."[14] We look to the saints to teach us how to live the life of Christ, to continue Christ's saving work in our broken world, to love and serve the One who was and is and is to come.

This chapter recognizes the saints of Advent. Their assigned dates, unless otherwise stated, are the anniversary of their death on earth. Many dates commemorate more than one person, since this is a collection derived from nearly 2,000 years of Christianity, as made explicit on the Roman Catholic, Byzantine and Anglican liturgical calendars. The symbols represent the unity of the date. The major saints days and 'O' antiphons should always be included on your calendar. Therefore, the permanent 1½"-by-4" symbol pictured within the text and numbered and lettered with a "P" is provided for placement on the rectangular base of the date blocks (see directions in chapter 9, section 7.F).

A summary suggestion is offered on each date for daily life application and is followed by a prayer to be used with the Advent wreath devotional (p. 31).

Keep alert and always persevere in supplication for all the saints.
—Ephesians 6:18

November 27–December 16: Advent Watchers and Holy Ones

November 27: Maximus, Bishop (462)

The earliest opening of the Advent season, November 27, remembers a French monk, Maximus, who was born into affluence and charm. Recognizing the shallowness of his favored life in Provence, France, Maximus distributed his riches to the poor and entered the monastery of Lerins. He became the abbot in 426, and for seven years the monastery thrived under his gentle, charismatic rule. In 433, the see of Reiz became vacant, and Maximus was elected bishop against his will. Yet, he humbly served the church with generosity and self-sacrifice.

For you know the generous act of our Lord Jesus Christ, that though he was rich, yet for your sakes he became poor, so that by his poverty you might become rich.
—2 Corinthians 8:9

The opening of Advent calls us to prepare our hearts with generous spirits of goodwill toward all. Our focus this week is to watch and take notice of our possessions. Awareness of our worldly attachments helps to lessen our desires and to increase space in our hearts for Christ. What attachment (attitude, person, thing) do you have that takes up space in your heart? Today, this week, watch that attachment. Do not judge it or try to discard it. Simply take notice of what role it plays in your life, and allow awareness to loosen its grip.

Prayer. Gracious God, thank you for the gentle generosity of Bishop Maximus. Watch with us, that we might see the attachments that fill our hearts and displace you from our lives. By awareness, we are set free to welcome you. Amen. Come, Lord Jesus.

Use Symbol 21. Since today can only be the First Sunday of Advent, if it is on the calendar at all, the day is marked with one lit candle on the Advent wreath.

November 28: Kamehameha and Emma,
King and Queen of Hawaii (1864, 1865)

King Kamehameha IV and his wife, Emma, ascended the Hawaiian throne in the wake of the 1854 smallpox epidemic. Concerned for the suffering people, they built Queen's Hospital. The king and queen aligned their royalty to the royalty of Christ and set out to serve the people rather than exercise earthly power.

Having been moved by an Anglican service in England when a young boy, the king asked the bishop of Oxford to send missionaries to establish the Anglican church in Hawaii. A month after the missionaries' arrival, October 11, 1862, the king and queen were confirmed into the church. They worked to build a cathedral and a school and to translate parts of *The Book of Common Prayer* and hymnal into their language. In 1864, a year after the death of his only child, the king died of a broken heart. The queen relinquished the throne and dedicated her life to serving the poor and the sick.[15]

Refusing worldly power invites participation in the sovereignty of Christ through service. Jesus begins and ends his earthly reign on an ass: into Bethlehem, within Mary's womb, to await birth; into Egypt, with Mary and Joseph, to hide from Herod's threats; and into Jerusalem, alone, to be crucified. The ass reminds us of the meekness and humility of our eternal king. Watch for an opportunity today to serve someone. For example, offer your place in line to someone coping with age, young children, or worry; or call, write or visit someone who is homebound or lonely.

Prayer. Gracious God, watch with us so that, like Kamehameha and Emma, we might see those opportunities to serve you by serving others, and

"Tell the daughter of Zion, Look your king is coming to you, humble, and mounted on a donkey, and on a colt, the foal of a donkey."
—Matthew 21:5

Symbol 32

fill our opened hearts with a generosity of quiet service to those we easily over-look. By awareness, we are set free to serve you. Amen. Come, Lord Jesus.

Symbol 32. The ass, associated with the birth of Jesus (see Symbol 36), represents the generous rule of Kamehameha and Emma when it is adorned with a lei around its neck.

November 29: Dorothy Day (1980)

An agnostic journalist for social justice, Dorothy Day discovered life in Christ through the loving kindness of Catholic sisters who cared for her while she was pregnant with her only child, Tamar. The acceptance of Christ and the Catholic faith cost Dorothy her relationship with Tamar's father. Yet, Christ consistently sent community to Dorothy to support her Christian vocation. During the Depression, a homeless man, Peter Maurin, approached Dorothy to begin a newspaper that called for Christian social justice. Awake to the opportunity, Dorothy birthed *The Catholic Worker*, which inspired a community of volunteers to serve the poor. With the sup-port of Peter and the homeless community, Dorothy sheltered and fed the homeless of New York, relying on God's providence to cover expenses. The success of the Catholic Worker House of Hospitality became a model for the opening of associate houses across the United States.

Dorothy Day took literally Jesus' injunction to be in solidarity with the poor. She found Christ particularly present in the homeless, and when she served them she served Christ face to face. With the keen insight of Isaiah, she saw the suffering Christ in society's outcasts; with the Spirit that inspired John the Baptist, she was outspoken and courageous on behalf of the poor; with the humility of Mary, she engaged in daily prayer to enable God's will to be done on earth.

Feeding the poor and caring for the destitute feeds and embraces Christ. Who and where are the outcasts, the unlovable, the homeless and the hun-gry in your community? What can you do this Advent season to love, serve and strengthen them? Set a plan of action and write it into one of the pock-ets on your calendar to assure its fulfillment.

Prayer. Merciful God, thank you for the example of Dorothy Day. Set our hearts aflame with your love, and quicken our hands with your compassion to care for the unlovable. By awareness, we are enabled to see you face to face and become servants to all. Amen. Come, Lord Jesus.

Symbol 33. The symbol of *The Catholic Worker* was designed in 1935 by Ade Bethune for the May issue of *The Catholic Worker*. The two figures stand in solidarity, united in Christ. In 1985, Ade revised the masthead to incor-porate the woman: a mother and agricultural worker.

"When you give a banquet, invite the poor, the crippled, the lame, and the blind."
—Luke 14:13

Symbol 33

November 30: Andrew the Apostle

Pope Gregory adopted St. Andrew's day to open Advent. Gregory decreed that the season of Advent was to last approximately four weeks, beginning on the Sunday closest to the feast of St. Andrew. Andrew opens Advent with a call to let go of possessions. Rather than joining the frenetic activity that crowds our lives during the season, we are bid to simplify, let go, and focus on who is coming, the One who instructs us to leave our nets and "follow me" (Matthew 4:19).

Originally a follower of John the Baptist, Andrew was the first disciple called by Jesus and he directly brought the news of Christ's presence to his brother Simon. The first disciple of Jesus and the first missionary for Christ, Andrew has the first major feast of the church year.

Andrew's recognition of Christ radically transformed his life, and his immediate response to follow Jesus models for us our call to follow Christ in our daily lives. Having found abundant life in Jesus, Andrew later perceived potential abundance in a boy's meager provisions. When Jesus sought bread for the thousands who needed food, Andrew offered, "There is a boy here who has five barley loaves and two fish. But what are they among so many people?" (John 6:9) Enough! More than enough—twelve baskets too much. Scarcity did not blind Andrew to the transformative power of Jesus, and his fetching the boy enabled the miracle of the loaves and fishes. When we offer our small provisions to Christ, we too enable people to be fed and to recognize Jesus.

Traditions about Andrew focus on his missionary work, particularly in Scythia (southern Russia), Greece and Scotland: countries that claim the patronage of Andrew. Lore holds that he was condemned to death by Proconsul Aegeas of Patras in Achaia because Andrew angered him with his preaching. The final straw was Andrew's converting Aegeas' wife, Maximilla, who then refused marital intimacy for as long as Aegeas remained a pagan. Andrew was bound to a cross with a rope and hung for two days before dying.

Andrew's radical following of Christ challenges us to trust God. Following Christ involves discipline—to listen to God when we pray, to watch for opportunities to follow Christ, to be ready to set aside everything for Christ. Today, watch for an opportunity to follow Jesus. Then reflect: were you willing to drop everything to follow? How might you be better prepared to follow tomorrow? Make watching for and following Christ a part of your Advent discipline.

Prayer. Loving God, may we, like Andrew, recognize your arrival, hear your call and follow you without delay. Help us to avoid worldly ensnarements; accept by grace the offering of our meager lives, and liberate our hands to serve you wholly. By awareness, we are set free to welcome you. Amen. Come, Lord Jesus.

Discipline your-selves, keep alert.

—1 Peter 5:8

Symbol 34/P-1

Symbol 34/P-1. The saltire, or "X"-shaped cross, reminds us that the cost of discipleship is high: Andrew put Christ first and became like Christ, even dying on a cross. A white cross tells of Andrew's love for Christ. It is encased in the blue of the heavens from which Christ comes (34); Andrew was a fisherman called by Jesus to "fish for people" (Mark 1:16–18) (P-1).

December 1: Nahum (c. 612 B.C.E.), Nicholas Ferrar (1637) and Rosa Parks

Nahum prophesied the end of the Assyrian domination of the Near East during the violent seventh century B.C.E. The fall of Assyria was a source of great joy for the Israelites, who longed for peace and the blessings of freedom. A cruelly enslaved Israel is consoled by Nahum, who encourages them to persevere: watch for and expect God's justice in spite of overwhelming discouragement; God will redeem the faithful. Nahum's prophesy of the day of the Lord originates one of the key messianic prophesies in Isaiah, contained in Isaiah's hymn to a new Jerusalem:

> How beautiful upon the mountains are the feet of the messenger who announces peace, who brings good news, who announces salvation, who says to Zion, "Your God reigns." —ISAIAH 52:7

Look! On the mountains the feet of one who brings good tidings, who proclaims peace! —Nahum 1:15

Symbol 35

Nicholas Ferrar, at the turn of the seventeenth century, encouraged the perseverance of faith during the upheaval of the Reformation. Ferrar founded a religious community at Little Gidding, Huntingdonshire, England, which maintained a focused life of daily prayer, meditation and fasting. Ferrar taught children, minded the needs of neighboring households, and wrote stories on Christian faith and life. The example of Ferrar and the Little Gidding community inspired T. S. Eliot's *Four Quartets*, rich in Advent imagery.

On December 1, 1955, Rosa Parks refused to surrender her bus seat to a white man. Her courage began to unravel the white oppression of the black community, particularly the Southern system of unjust laws and practices. Parks' quiet refusal to have her dignity demeaned inspired Martin Luther King, Jr., to help organize the black community's boycott of the Montgomery, Alabama, buses; in one year the buses were desegregated. The simple yet courageous action of Rosa Parks strengthened the civil rights movement across the United States, and it teaches us that daily behavior is the means of justice for all.

Three people, spanning centuries and continents, reflect God's Advent. Nahum prophesies the Incarnation of the Prince of Peace who comes for our salvation; Nicholas Ferrar recognizes and serves the presence of Christ in his neighbors; Rosa Parks expects the day of the Lord when God's justice is fully actualized. We, the body of Christ here and now, are called to enact the servant ministry of Jesus, to resist oppression and practice the love of God courageously in our daily lives. What simple action can you take today to offer respect for a fellow human being?

Prayer. Gracious God, thank you for the witness of Nahum, Nicholas Ferrar and Rosa Parks. Be with us now and grant us perception to confess you and courage to resist oppression. Teach us to recognize you in the people we encounter daily and to respond with the love that respects all. Lead us in your grace until that day when you come in glory. By awareness, we are set free to welcome you. Amen. Come, Lord Jesus.

Symbol 35. Many Christmas cards sent during Advent depict a lion and a lamb with the inscription "Peace on Earth." The symbol comes from Isaiah's vision of God incarnate, who ushers in the reign of peace and justice (Isaiah 11:6–9). When the lion, a symbol of power and courage, lies reconciled with the lamb, a symbol of meekness and innocent suffering, we are assured that evil will be vanquished and cosmic harmony will prevail.

If it seems to tarry, wait for it; it will surely come, it will not delay.
—*Habakkuk 2:3*

Symbol 36

December 2: Habakkuk (c. 598 B.C.E.), Channing Moore Williams (1910) and the Martyrs of El Salvador (1980)

The Hebrew prophet, Habakkuk, was deeply concerned for the suffering of others. Why, he asks, is a just God silent in the face of evil? God reassures Habakkuk that God's justice and righteousness will reign triumphantly, though not yet. In the meantime, "the righteous [must] live by their faith" (2:4). God assures us that things are not as they appear. The faithful do prevail and the unrighteous perish. Habakkuk's prayer of praise hopes for the Messiah, who comes to save the people "in the midst of the years" (3:2 NKJV).

An early translation of the Hebrew scriptures, the Septuagint, translates this verse to read *in medio duorum animalium*, "between two beasts you are known," the origin of the tradition of the Messiah's birth in a manger between an ass and an ox.[16] The tradition continues that the ass and the ox accompanied the holy family on their flight into Egypt. The ass carried Mary and Jesus, while the ox, led by Joseph, packed their belongings. Like the ass and the ox, who readily carried the Christ Child into unfamiliar land, the figures we remember today perceived Christ in their midst and responded by carrying Christ into foreign lands.

Channing Moore Williams was an Anglican missionary bishop who carried the word of God into China and Japan. An American, ordained a deacon in 1866, Williams left for China, where he was ordained a priest in 1857. In 1859 he continued on to Japan, and in 1866, he was elected bishop to China and Japan. When Japan opened its doors to the West in 1868, he focused his ministry in Japan, where he founded a university and missions and translated *The Book of Common Prayer*. In 1908, he returned to his home, Richmond, Virginia, where he died on December 2, 1910.

Recently, four American women, concerned for the oppression of the poor in Central America, took their joy and hope in Christ to the Salvadoran people. Ursuline Sister Dorothy Kazel, Maryknoll lay worker Jean Donovan and Maryknoll Sisters Maura Clarke and Ita Ford fed, taught, nursed and sheltered the poor. On December 2, 1980, the four women were abducted and shot to death. These servants of Christ, like the suffering servant, were dealt unjust deaths because they brought hope and justice to a desperate people. In the face of their innocent suffering, we lament with Habakkuk:

> O LORD, how long shall [we] cry for help, and you will not listen? Or cry to you "Violence!" and you will not save? —HABAKKUK 1:2

Come and save your people!

The life, labors and zeal of Habakkuk, Channing Moore Williams and the Martyrs of El Salvador are signs of God's passion to be with us. Faith endures through the ages when witnesses who trust God work for healing and reconciliation in a broken world. We, too, are to be a shining light to an oppressed world. How can you relieve a burden from a friend, loved one or stranger to lighten his or her heart at Christmas?

Prayer. Compassionate God, with Habakkuk, Channing Moore Williams and the Martyrs of El Salvador, we watch for you and your answer. Faithfully, we wait patiently for you to come. Help us to set aside our fears, and accord us your grace to herald your coming reign of peace and justice. By awareness, we are set free to welcome you. Amen. Come, Lord Jesus.

Symbol 36. The ox and the ass are traditional figures of the Nativity. The ox was the sacrificial animal in Old Testament times, and Jesus is Isaiah's suffering servant, sacrificed for our salvation. The ass represents the humble birth of our Lord and the degradation he endured when he revealed God's love for us. Together they reveal Christ in our midst and our commission to servant ministry at any cost.

The great day of the LORD is near, near and hastening fast.
—Zephaniah 1:14

December 3: Zephaniah (609 B.C.E.) and Francis Xavier (1552)

Today is the latest date to begin the Advent season. Zephaniah urgently warns that the day of the Lord is quickly upon us. Repent now, for soon it will be too late! The prophet tells of a light that will penetrate the darkness, a lantern that will search Jerusalem for the obedient and humble followers of God. Those found worthy, the *anawim*, the humble and lowly of the land (2:3, 3:12), will be guests of honor on that day.

Symbol 37

Zephaniah (meaning "Yahweh protects"), perceiving the day of the Lord, wrote during the reign of Josiah (640–609 B.C.E.), a king who was instrumental in the religious reforms of Judah (2 Kings 22–23, 2 Chronicles 34–35). Zephaniah warned against religious syncretism, idolatry and pride and described a day of doom for all people because the day of judgment is universal. Beyond judgment is God's mercy: hope and consolation are offered to those who wait vigilantly, serving God with humble and contrite hearts. They will be forgiven and gathered home with great rejoicing.

Francis Xavier is an example of solid service to Christ by self-sacrifice. Gentle and courteous, he chose to live in solidarity with the poor. He was born into the nobility of Navarra, Spain, in 1506. In 1525 he left to attend a university in Paris, where he became a close friend of Ignatius of Loyola. With Ignatius and three other colleagues, he helped found the Society of Jesus (the Jesuits) in 1534. Moved to take the Christian message to those who had never heard it, Xavier embarked on missionary service to India, Ceylon, the Philippines and Japan. He shared the gospel through his care for the poor, the lame and the outcast across those lands. Xavier died en route to China and is remembered as the patron saint of the East Indies and foreign missions.

Advent calls us to wait for the day of the Lord by taking courage and living the way of Christ—not the ways of the world—in preparation for our homecoming and the reign of peace and justice. Today, share the love and hope of Christ with someone feeling sick, sad or lonely. Offer words and deeds of kindness.

Prayer. Merciful God, with Zephaniah and Francis Xavier, we watch for you with obedient and humble hearts. Help us to share the hope of your gospel in our world; by your grace may we be found worthy of your kingdom at the sending out of your light across the lands. By awareness, we are set free to welcome you. Amen. Come, Lord Jesus.

Symbol 37. Francis Xavier is depicted with a tonsure and having a short, black beard. He holds a cross to represent his missionary zeal; the lantern reminds us that God will search our hearts with the light of Christ on the day of the Lord.

December 4: Barbara (third century) and John of Damascus (760)

Unwavering courage and devotion, even in the face of suffering, mark the life of Barbara, a third-century martyr. Barbara was the daughter of a rich noble, Diocorus, who forbade her to marry. Since she was appealing, he locked her in a tower so no man could behold her beauty. Barbara used her solitary confinement to study philosophy, and thereby determined the existence of one God. A Christian, disguised as a doctor, gained entrance to the tower and augmented her belief in one God. When her father discovered her conversion to Christianity, he had her tortured. When she refused to renounce her faith, Diocorus beheaded Barbara. Legend tells us that at the moment she died, lightning struck with a loud crack and killed Diocorus, making Barbara the patron saint of thunderstorms and explosions. Because of her courageous devotion to Christ, even when tortured, she is also the patron of illness and good death. During the epidemic illnesses and deaths caused by the Black Plague in Europe (1347–1351) Barbara was invoked as one of the Fourteen Holy Helpers.

The feast of St. Barbara marks the opening of the Christmas season in Syria and Lebanon. Instead of having a Christmas tree, the Syrians decorate a table with colorful candles, pastries and candies. A party is held and wheat cakes commemorating the dead and symbolizing immortality are shared. From the party, children are sent out to treat the poor with the candies and pastries. In Germany, "Barbara twigs" are cut from fruit or nut trees and kept watered in a warm place in hopes of blooms at Christmas. This tradition follows the legend that all trees blossomed and bore fruit on the night Christ was born.

John of Damascus was an eighth-century monk at the monastery of St. Sabas, near Jerusalem. In 726, the same year John was ordained priest, Byzantine Emperor Leo the Isaurian published an edict forbidding the use of holy images and ordered the destruction of all religious art. John wrote enthusiastically in defense of holy images, explaining that the images were not idols since they did not try to image God, but imaged the humanity of Christ in Jesus and the saints. When we reject religious art, we reject the Incarnation of God. The Seventh Ecumenical Council (787) adopted John's thesis: it is appropriate to venerate icons, but worship God alone.

Barbara and John of Damascus teach us about Advent vigilance. Often we are faced with decisions that may go against popular or national belief. We need to watch our behavior and have the courage, like Barbara and John, to express and observe God's loving kindness and mercy, even if it isolates us from accepted ideas and behavior. Advent challenges us to be outcasts for Christ. Spend some quiet time today with a work of art in a church or museum, outdoors or in your home. Does the image enhance your love for God? How? Or cut a branch to tend and watch during the next few weeks. Let the branch remind you of the need to pay wakeful attention to God.

Prayer. Creator God, with Barbara and John of Damascus, we watch for you with courageous and devoted hearts. Open our eyes to recognize you in creation, that we may discern what is of you and what is not. Thank you for artists whose works help us to see creation afresh and deepen our faith. By awareness, we are set free to welcome you. Amen. Come, Lord Jesus.

Symbol 38. A story tells that a Moslem caliph cut off John's hand and nailed it to the city gate as a warning to others who defended holy images.

Keep alert, stand firm in your faith, be courageous, be strong. Let all that you do be done in love.
—1 Corinthians 16:13–14

Symbol 38

Mary miraculously rejoined John's hand out of gratitude for his zest and defense of her images. Our symbol today is a severed hand that is nailed to Barbara's tower. It reminds us of the cost of discipleship when we persevere in faith.

December 5: Clement of Alexandria (c. 210)

Gnosticism, an early Christian heresy that valued gnosis (Greek "knowledge") as the source of redemption, held that secret knowledge possessed only by a select few saved them from the fallen world. They believed that creation, inherently evil, was beyond redemption because it was created by an inferior deity and that Christ, the redeemer, did not genuinely become flesh or suffer death on the cross.

Clement of Alexandria, Egypt, was a Greek philosopher who became a defender of the Christian faith against Gnosticism and intellectualism. Clement maintained that true gnosis was available to all through the scriptures. Clement's writings were important to the Christian cause among the intellectual circles of Alexandria because he was able to develop a positive relationship between Christianity and Greek culture. Clement applied the Gospel of Mark's story of the rich man (10:17–31) to fight anti-materialism and intellectualism. Like wealth, philosophy and intellectual thought are not necessarily enemies of the faith but may be used fruitfully to serve Christianity. While we honor many saints who renounce their wealth and literally "sell all and give to the poor," Clement opens the door for those who are not called to a literal renunciation of wealth but to its right use.

What do you own or want that would crush you if it were lost, damaged or not received? Thinking of that object, say to yourself, "My happiness does not depend on _____." This practice will help release you from its possession.

Clement made the first recorded mention of a Christmas celebration. Tonight is the eve of the feast of St. Nicholas. Many children worldwide leave a shoe at their door before retiring in hopes of St. Nick's visit. If you observe this tradition, be mindful that Nicholas is an example of the right use of wealth.

Prayer. Gracious God, we wait vigilantly for your arrival. Thank you for your servant Clement of Alexandria and for the gift of our intellects. Teach us to trust you, and release us from our possessions so that we may use them in service of you at all times. By awareness, we are set free to welcome you. Amen. Come, Lord Jesus.

Symbol 39. The Greek cross with arms of equal length reminds us of Christ's faithful servant Clement, who taught that two interpretations of the parable of the rich man are of equal value. Either literally or liberally, we are charged to put our intellectual and material wealth into service for Christ.

"Go, sell what you own, and give the money to the poor, and you will have treasure in heaven; then come, follow me."
—Mark 10:21

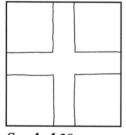

Symbol 39

December 6: Nicholas, Bishop of Myra (c. 342)

The right use of wealth is exemplified by Nicholas, the bishop of Myra. He gave money anonymously, displaying God's mercy with the sole desire that people would praise and glorify God. Nicholas lived in Asia Minor during the Diocletian persecutions (284–305). The Emperor Diocletian had him tortured and imprisoned; his release was granted when Constantine became emperor in 306. He may have participated at the First Ecumenical Council of Nicea in 325. Byzantine Emperor Justinian (483–565) honored Nicholas as a saint in the East, and when some of his relics were moved to Bari, Italy, in 1087, his veneration became popular in the West. Legends about Nicholas flourished, effectively making him the most popular saint in the world, without regard to fact or fiction. Here are a few of his most enduring legends.

Nicholas was born into wealth, yet even as a child he gave money and clothes to the poor. When he was old enough, he gave away his inheritance. In all cases, he gave to promote God's glory, not his own.

Perhaps most popular is the story that when an impoverished neighbor was distraught because he could not support or offer a dowry for his three daughters, the neighbor resolved to sell his daughters into prostitution or slavery (the legend varies). Nicholas, moved by their predicament, secretly threw bags of coins through their window for three consecutive nights. The neighbor was relieved and overjoyed, since the amount in the bags met each girl's dowry. Some legends say that the coins landed in the girls' stockings, hung by the fire to dry, originating the custom of hanging Christmas stockings on the hearth.

Nicholas is the patron of children because of the legends that he brought healing and life back to children. A popular story tells that when three young boys were en route to visit Bishop Nicholas, they stopped overnight at a tavern. The innkeeper, poor and in dire need for meat for his customers, killed the boys, chopped them up and soaked them in brine. Once the salted flesh was cured, he planned to serve it to his customers. Nicholas, warned in a dream about the repulsive crime, rushed to the tavern and brought the boys back to life.

Seafarers and sailors honor Nicholas as their patron because he frequently helped mariners lost in storms find their way to land. Harbor churches throughout the world are dedicated to Nicholas, who was bishop in a coastal diocese (Myra).

The veneration of saints was abolished in parts of Europe under the Reformation (1500–1700), with the result that the festival of St. Nicholas was widely forgotten beyond Catholic circles. Only the Protestant Dutch retained the custom of the visit of St. Nicholas, due to his patronage of seafarers. And by way of the Dutch, Santa Claus was born in America.

"Let the little children come to me, and do not stop them; for it is to such as these that the kingdom of heaven belongs."
—Matthew 19:14

Symbol P-2

Symbol 40

Symbol 41

How sweet are your words to my taste, sweeter than honey to my mouth!
—Psalm 119:103

Symbol 42

Settled in New Amsterdam, their American colony, the Dutch celebrated the day of *Sinter Klaas* (pronounced "Santa Claus") on December 6. When the English took over the colony, naming it New York, they preferred the Dutch gift bearer to their own Father Christmas. The English, to the delight of their children, adopted Sinter Klaas to suit their Presbyterian conventions. Rather than a sainted bishop, the new Santa Claus came as a deliveryman for Christ on December 24. This corresponds with the German Lutheran *Christkindel*, developed by Martin Luther. To lessen the importance of Saint Nicholas, Luther substituted a gift-bearing Christ Child who comes on December 24. Realizing Nicholas' popularity, he instituted the idea that Nicholas is merely a messenger that passes on requests for presents to the Christ Child.

This day, we celebrate not Santa Claus but the historic bishop of Myra, Nicholas. His feast comes early in Advent to remind us to repent and prepare our hearts for the Christ Child's arrival. Today, when Nicholas comes to expose our behavior, pardon the repentant and fill our shoes with gifts, we anticipate the final coming of Christ at the Last Judgment. Those who refuse to repent find coal or a switch in their shoe, left by Nicholas' attendant devil, *Krampus*. To honor Nicholas today, write a confession and place it in the fire to signify the Light that exposes and forgives sin. Then write your Christmas list in remembrance of Nicholas, a messenger for Christ, and place it in your stocking to hang until Christmas. Members of the family may sneak in to read the lists for ideas to make shopping easier.

Prayer. Merciful God, we expect your coming—today into our hearts, on Christmas Day humbly enfleshed, at the last day in glory. Thank you for the example of Bishop Nicholas of Myra. Reveal to us where we have failed to serve and love you so that we may repent and prepare our hearts to welcome you. Free us from greed and simplify our needs. By awareness, we are set free to welcome you. Amen. Come, Lord Jesus.

Symbols P-2/40/41. The bishop blesses and leads us to Christ (P-2); three stockings hang open for God's gifts (40); an anchor with three money bags represents hope grounded in faith on which the right use of wealth hangs (41).

December 7: Ambrose, Bishop of Milan (397)

Ambrose, son of a Roman governor, became governor in northern Italy in 373 when the Arian controversy was threatening orthodox Christian belief. (Arianism rejected the divinity of Jesus on the grounds that God is unknowable and separate from creation, Jesus was a created being and thus not fully divine, and the incarnate Christ did not assume a human soul and thus was not fully human.) When the see of Milan became vacant, the Arians and Catholics argued bitterly over whom to elect bishop. Ambrose intervened to reconcile the two factions with the result that both groups exclaimed,

"Ambrose shall be bishop!" Though raised Christian, Ambrose was not baptized. Directly, he was baptized and ordained bishop on December 7, 373.

Bishop Ambrose was an astute defender of orthodox belief and an effective hymnodist. He wrote practical lessons to educate people on the Christian faith and introduced antiphonal (verse-by-verse alternation) chanting to worship. Theological wisdom earned Ambrose the title "Doctor of the Church." The eloquence of his writings moved Augustine, who would also become a doctor of the church, to convert to Christianity.

Ambrose believed that the earth belonged to everyone, that the rich were to share with the poor and that peace and justice were to be practiced at all costs. With a steadfast faith that was fearless of imperial power, Ambrose forced Emperor Theodosius to perform public penance for the massacre of thousands in Thessalonika in 390. Watching our own motives, we can notice where out of fear of worldly opinion we stray from the ways of God. An awareness of our motives will help us to overcome our fears and to follow God with courage. Be mindful of the *why* of your actions. Catch yourself when you are tempted to yield to temporal voices. Without judging, shine a light on the temptation and watch it dissipate.

Prayer. "Lord Jesus Christ, you are for me medicine when I am sick; you are my strength when I need help; you are life itself when I fear death; you are the way when I long for heaven; you are light when all is dark; you are my food when I need nourishment."[17] By awareness, we are set free to welcome you. Amen. Come, Lord Jesus.

Symbol 42. The beehive identifies Ambrose because when he was a baby a swarm of bees hovered over his lips. The event foretold his verbal eloquence with words as sweet as honey. The beehive is also a symbol for the church community that works together for the benefit of all.

December 8: Immaculate Conception of the Virgin Mary

The feast of the Immaculate Conception reminds us that Mary, the mother of God, is pure and radiates God's grace. Her faithful obedience to God leads us from the wayward path of sin back to the righteous path of God. Mary, the new Eve, exemplifies a grace-filled relationship with God instead of an antagonistic relationship with evil.

The feast of the Immaculate Conception, which evolved out of popular piety and tradition, is essentially a people's feast that celebrates love and devotion for Mary. The official doctrine of the church originated in the Eastern church during the eighth century. The feast was instituted in the West in 1476, though it did not receive formal status until December 8, 1854, when Pope Pius IX defined the doctrine. It teaches that Mary was free from original sin at the moment of her conception. This special grace is a gift

[Gabriel] came to her and said, "Greetings favored one! The Lord is with you."
—Luke 1:28

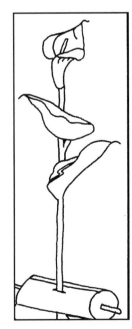

Symbol P-3

from God that prepared her to become the mother of God. The date of December 8 is set nine months before her alleged birthday, September 8.

The Immaculate Conception has been a subject of controversy from its beginning. Augustine of Hippo (354–430) exempted Mary from actual but not original sin. Franciscan Duns Scotus (1265–1308) defended the doctrine stating, "what is possible, what is appropriate, is done." Regardless, Mary is a humble servant of God, the first and model disciple of the gospel,[18] who expectantly completed and welcomed the coming of Christ in the flesh. Today, how might you be a God-bearer? Conclude your Advent devotional with "The Magnificat" (p. 25).

Customary Prayer. "Hail Mary, full of grace, the Lord is with you; blessed are you among women, and blessed is the fruit of your womb, Jesus. Holy Mary, Mother of God, pray for us sinners, now and at the hour of our death." Amen. Come, Lord Jesus.

Symbol 18/P-3. Traditionally, the woman clothed with the sun who tramples the head of a dragon (Revelation 12:1–6) is a symbol for the Immaculate Conception. To emphasize the common, ordinary Mary, who faithfully expected and welcomed God, we use the woman reading scripture from chapter 3 (18); the lily grows through the Torah and reminds us of her purity (P-3).

"Their voice has gone out to all the earth, and their words to the ends of the world."
—*Romans 10:18*

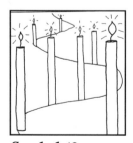

Symbol 43

December 9: The Holy Men [and Women] of the Old Testament

Advent keenly echoes and identifies with the faith of the Old Testament and participates in its longing for the coming of the Messiah. Advent, by way of the Hebrew scriptures, sets our hearts aflame for the coming of Christ as we discover the identity of Jesus. In short, the Old Testament is the context and content of Advent.

The liturgical calendar celebrates a number of Old Testament figures during Advent: Nahum, Habakkuk and Zephaniah during the first week; Haggai, Daniel and Esther during the second and third weeks; and Adam and Eve on Christmas Eve. Although special days of observance are not reserved for other Old Testament figures, they clearly exemplify Advent vigilance and expectation. Isaiah is the decisive Old Testament figure that embodies messianic longing and heralds the coming of Emmanuel (see Symbol 17). Amos, Baruch, and Zechariah urge us to vigilantly prepare for the day of the Lord (see Symbols 13 and 15). Illumined by God, these and many other Old Testament figures announce the coming of the Redeemer.

Today, we mark the rich heritage of faith that ushers in the Advent of Christ. Discuss the importance of the Hebrew scriptures to your faith. Share a character that is particularly meaningful to you. Consider the question, what is a prophet?

Prayer. Merciful God, attentive to your word, we journey with expectant hope on the path illuminated by your people, Israel. The prophets call us to repent and prepare the way for our salvation. Come quickly with your grace and mercy to help us repent and joyfully recognize the arrival of Christ in a manger, in our hearts, and in glory. Expectant, we long to welcome you. Amen. Come, Lord Jesus.

Symbol 43. The holy figures of the Old Testament, whose courage and perception prepare the way for God's Advent, are like a series of candles getting brighter through time.

December 10: Thomas Merton (1968) and
International Human Rights Day (1948)

Thomas Merton is a quintessential Advent person. "Watch! Wake up!" his writings charge. Seek God now and always; do not rely on complacent Western answers to "happiness." They are empty and worthless illusions. Many have sold their (divine) birthright for a mess of societal, cultural and religious porridge. Reflect, pray, meditate. See through the screens, the cheapness, the inadequacy of anything less than the living God who now comes. Merton's Advent vision of keen truth exposes the foibles of twentieth-century society and religion.

Seek the LORD and his strength; seek his presence continually.
—Psalm 105:4

Born in France and orphaned when a teenager, Merton wandered first to Cambridge University in England then to Columbia University in New York, where he earned a degree in journalism. He dabbled in communism until he discovered and converted to the Catholic faith. After teaching and working with the poor in New York, Merton entered the Trappist monastery at Gethsemani Abbey, Kentucky. Home at last but never at ease, Merton watched for Christ with vigilant awareness and a clarity of vision. His death by accidental electrocution on December 10, 1968, came "like a thief in the night," yet like the wise bridesmaids of Matthew, he was ready with oil in his lamp.

Symbol 44

Prayer, work and study were Merton's rule of life, and they are embodied in his prolific and poignant writings, which expose the illusions of the world with prophetic power. Rightly, his writings, spanning nearly thirty years, are markings for many current seekers of God. Merton valued listening to all points of view and became a leader in ecumenism and world peace. Even his untimely death is couched in his seeking and willingness "to see"—he was in Asia as a pilgrim monk from the West seeking bridges to Eastern monasticism and Buddhism—that the reign of Christ is here now.

Bridge building is critical in our shrinking world. Today marks the anniversary of the United Nations' adoption of the Universal Declaration of Human Rights, which recognizes thirty basic human rights essential to all people. The United Nations advocates fundamental human freedoms and urges citizens worldwide to do the same. What can you do today to promote a humane life for someone whose humanity is consistently denied? Try listening with an open heart to a point of view different from your own. How can that viewpoint expand your horizons, promote human freedom and lead you into a deeper encounter with God?

Prayer. Merciful God, prepare our hearts by the grace of your Holy Spirit to seek and find you in our brothers and sisters; pour your love through us to bring light to the world, and open our eyes and ears to receive your love from others; grant us knowledge of you here and now. Expectant, we long to welcome you. Amen. Come, Lord Jesus.

Symbol 44. The lotus is one of the richest symbols of Buddhism. It is the mystic center of the world, nature's womb, which unites all the elements of the world and from which true human potential emerges. A symbol of birth and creation, the lotus corresponds to the Christmas rose, symbolic of the Nativity in the West (pictured in symbols P-11, 55 and 64). The "jewel in the lotus" presented in Buddhism is, for us, the Christ Child. The lotus–Christmas rose, a unifying symbol of Buddhism and Christianity, symbolizes the world unity that was embodied in Merton's life and that is necessary to human rights.

December 12: Our Lady of Guadalupe

On December 9, 1531, an impoverished Aztec Indian, Juan Diego, was walking in Mexico's countryside when a young woman clothed in traditional royal Aztec attire appeared to him. "Build a church here, where I stand, so that I may be a source of consolation to the people," she instructed Juan.

Juan took the woman's message to the local Catholic bishop, but the bishop refused to believe him. Juan returned to the spot and again the woman appeared, assuring Juan of his mission. Again the bishop refused to believe Juan; he demanded proof. On December 12, Juan returned to the site yet again. The woman guided Juan to a patch of roses that was miraculously growing in the barren cold of winter and instructed him to gather the roses into his cloak as a sign for the bishop. When he opened his cloak for the bishop, the woman's image was imprinted inside his cloak! The chapel was built and became one of the most popular shrines in North America.

The woman's appearance came during a time of brutality imposed on the Aztecs by the Spanish. The woman, Mary, brought a message of hope and consolation to these devastated people. Millions of Aztecs converted to Christianity and were baptized in celebration of God's love for the poor.

Our Lady of Guadalupe is the patroness of the Americas and her appearance is celebrated throughout the Americas today with singing, dancing,

The glory of the LORD shall be revealed, and all people shall see it together.
—Isaiah 40:5

Symbol 45

feasting, and great rejoicing, because God loves the poor and is the source of justice. Join in the celebration: attend a local festival and invite friends, or serve a Mexican dinner to them. Over the meal, discuss a time when God stopped you in your tracks. What message were you given? How was it received?

Prayer. Compassionate God, we your expectant people remember that you came to us poor and without a place to lay your head. With Our Lady Guadalupe, help us to remember all people who are poor, neglected and oppressed. Strengthen us to hear their message to us: that you are a God of love and justice. Have mercy on us and deliver us from participating in cruelty to our neighbors. Expectant, we long to welcome you. Amen. Come, Lord Jesus.

Symbol 45. This illustration of Our Lady of Guadalupe is based on the image found in the Basilica of Guadalupe, Mexico City. She is the queen of heaven and is wearing a crown and a red gown under a green cloak that is adorned with stars and surrounded by an aureole of the sun.

December 13: Lucy (304)

The feast of Lucy occurs during the Geminid meteor showers, sometimes called "St. Lucy's Lights." The northern sky filled with shooting stars prompts us to put on "the armor of light" in anticipation of the day of the Lord. Before the Gregorian calendar reform in 1582, the feast of *Santa Lucia* fell on the shortest day of the year. Lucy ("light") marked the close of the long, dark nights and heralded the new light to come. Thus her feast is identified with a wreath of candles to drive away the darkness and welcome the returning sunlight.

Born to nobility in Syracuse, Sicily, young Lucy accompanied her mother on a pilgrimage to the tomb of Agatha. Her mother was miraculously healed of her issue of blood, convincing Lucy to serve God. She gave all her riches to the poor and lived a life of service. She was beheaded after surviving extreme torture during the Diocletian persecutions. Her relics remain in Venice, Italy, at Santa Lucia Church.

Tales of a miraculous appearance of Lucy to a desperately hungry Sweden, her head haloed with light and her arms filled with enough food for everyone, generate the traditional "Lucia bride." In Swedish homes, at cockcrow, the eldest girl in the house dresses in a white gown sashed in red and crowns her head with an evergreen wreath of seven to nine candles to impersonate Lucy. The *Lussibrud* wakes all the sleepers with coffee, sweet drink and cakes called "Lucy cats." The cakes are circular swirls, like cinnamon buns, that represent the eternal Sun. All gather for breakfast and tales of Lucy, who announces that darkness is broken and the Son is coming.

The night is far gone, the day is near.
—*Romans 13:12*

Symbol 46

To honor Lucy and the Advent of the Light of the world, choose a family member to rise early and awaken the household with beverage and donuts or round sweet rolls. Just before dawn, you may want to go outside and try to spot the Geminid lights.

Prayer. God of light, thank you for Lucy's beautiful and grace-filled light. Help us to live like Lucy: devoted to you without wavering and loving others selflessly so that our self-sacrifice and service to the poor travels far.[19] Expectant, we long to welcome you. Amen. Come, Lord Jesus.

Symbol 46. The servant girl is crowned with a wreath of candles.

December 14: John of the Cross (1591)

Darkness consistently symbolizes evil, alienation from God, and death; yet the mysticism of John of the Cross teaches otherwise: darkness is the light! It is naked trust in God, holy detachment, the place where we penetrate our depths and discover the unknowable God. Honoring John of the Cross during Advent reminds us of the polarities and ambiguities of life—of life and death, of holy and evil, of joy and sorrow, of light and darkness. We live the mixture, daily faced with a choice: do we choose the will of God or the gratification of self?[20]

John of the Cross was a mystic who was born into village poverty in Castile, Spain. He was trained in the Christian faith by the Jesuits, and at age twenty he entered a Carmelite friary. Angered at the laxity of the Carmelites, John observed a strict rule and instituted a reform of the order. His "rebellion" earned him nine months of imprisonment. Locked in darkness, John birthed his collection of poetry, found in *The Spiritual Canticle*, about the way to God through contemplation, prayer and love. The mystic's writings are addressed to those called to the contemplative life. Whether the grace of contemplation nourishes our spirituality, we can learn from John of the Cross to depend wholly on God in faith and love. He teaches us to trust God and let all else fall where it will. And he tells us that if we sacrifice our will and desires to God, God will become our light, and if we plunge into the darkness of detachment, we will be enlightened. We must detach not only from possessions and relationships but also from our ideas about God and religious practices. Our desires and grasping, no matter how noble, lead only away from God. Dependence on God is free and effortless and comes solely by God's grace.

Learn detachment and quiet your too busy life by practicing daily awareness: determine to what or to whom you are attached (status, possessions, ideas, emotions, success, and so on) and say, "My happiness does not depend on _____."

Prayer. Merciful God, we hungrily feed upon the ways of the world; shine your searchlight onto our attachments, every one of which leads away from

The night is as bright as the day, for darkness is as light to you.
—Psalm 139:12

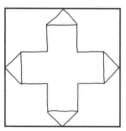

Symbol 47

you. Grant us the courage to enter the darkness with John of the Cross, where no attachment exists, and by your grace lead us into your everlasting light. Expectant, we long to welcome you. Amen. Come, Lord Jesus.

Symbol 47. The cross is white to represent John's purity of faith. The tips are red in remembrance of his persecution. The top half of the field is the black of darkness, and the lower half is the brown and white of the Carmelite habit.

December 16: Haggai (520 B.C.E.) and the Beginning of Las Posadas

In 538 B.C.E., Israel was released from its Babylonian captivity and allowed to return home. Haggai was the first prophet to inspire the people of Israel to unify their disrupted religious life, calling the people to prepare for the messianic age, an age of prosperity and abundance. Five addresses made over a three-month period brought about the reconstruction of the Temple and purification of worship. The rebuilt Temple was completed by 515 B.C.E.

The people of Israel journeyed from captivity back home in peace and hope. Today, we begin the final journey of hope for release from our captivity by sin. Surely when the Messiah comes we will be freed to find our home in God. The Mexican-American community commences *Las Posadas*: a nine-day reenactment of the journey Mary and Joseph made from Nazareth to Bethlehem, seeking shelter or hospitality. The nine days of devotion are called a "novena." The novena, introduced by Ignatius of Loyola (sixteenth century), recalls the nine-month pregnancy of Mary and the nine days between Christ's Ascension and the coming of the Spirit on the day of Pentecost that the apostles spent in prayer.

Las Posadas ("the Inns") dates from c. 1000, when medieval "miracle plays" depicted the birth of Christ to instruct and lead the people in worship. In Germany, the *Herbergsuchem* ("search for an inn") was a dramatic portrayal of Mary and Joseph's difficult search for shelter in Bethlehem. After many rejections, the couple finds shelter in a stable. John of the Cross, in 1580, adapted the German pageant to the monastic novena of prayer recited the nine days before Christmas. *Las Posadas* became popular throughout Hispanic Europe and was carried into Mexico by the Spanish missionaries. In 1587, Augustinian Friar Diego de Soria of Acolman, Mexico, instituted the novena for the holy child to combat the Aztec Indian worship of Huitzilopochtli, their god of war.

Today, *Las Posadas* initiates the Christmas festivities in Mexico and is celebrated in the Americas with prayer, song, feasting and games. The novena centers on two key themes from the gospel: the relentless rejection of Jesus by the arrogant and the joy that comes to the friends who welcome him.

Today, set up your Nativity scene but leave the manger empty and place Mary and Joseph (and the Magi) some distance away. Over the next nine

[God] executes justice for the orphan and the widow, and loves the strangers, providing them with food and clothing.
—Deuteronomy 10:18

Symbol 48

days, move Mary and Joseph closer and closer to the stable. On at least one evening between December 16 and 24, gather family, friends or church community to enact *Las Posadas*. Choose a gathering spot and then, led by youths dressed as an angel, Mary or Joseph, journey to three homes or rooms in the vicinity. At each door, stop the procession, ask for shelter and pray for the poor, the oppressed and the forgotten. The "innkeepers" behind the first three doors yell their refusal of hospitality. At a fourth door, or the church, the "innkeeper" welcomes all in for prayer and song around the empty manger. Fellowship follows with a Mexican fiesta and the breaking of a piñata.

Have all in the procession carry candles or flashlights to symbolize the stars that light the way to the place of the Savior's birth. The place of *Las Posadas* should be decorated with an empty manger, candles, greenery and flowers (poinsettias or roses). Gifts for the coming Christ Child may be offered for distribution to the needy of the community.

Prayer. Merciful God, forgive us when we reject you. Grant us grace to shelter the homeless and welcome the stranger into our homes and hearts, so that your coming may be a night of happiness and rejoicing because we gave hospitality to you. Expectant, we long to welcome you. Amen. Come, Lord Jesus.

Symbol 48. The Latin form of Haggai, Aggeus, was often confused with the Latin for angel, *angelus*. The angel carrying a candle reminds us of Haggai and of the angel who leads *Las Posadas* with the light of heaven and illumines the way to the Christ Child.

December 17–23: The Great 'O' Antiphons of Advent

Coming from the throne are flashes of lightning, and rumblings and peals of thunder, and in front of the throne burn seven flaming torches, which are the seven spirits of God.
—Revelation 4:5

Antiphons are short, focused verses that are recited before and after a psalm or canticle during a worship service. Usually, antiphons are from scripture, and they vary with the liturgical seasons, emphasizing the appointed theme of the day or season. Familiar to many are the Great 'O' antiphons of Advent because of the popular Advent hymn "O Come, O Come, Emmanuel," adapted from a fifteenth-century hymn by Thomas Helmore (1811–1890).

The Great 'O' antiphons of Advent are poignant prayers calling for and proclaiming the coming of Christ as they invoke Old Testament messianic titles. Their origins are unknown, but evidence of their use dates back to the ninth century. While variation of their number and use exists, traditionally, a succession of seven 'O' antiphons are sung individually from December 17 through December 23. They are recited to focus, introduce and conclude "The Magnificat" (p. 25), the ordinary canticle read during Evening Prayer. The assignment of the 'O' antiphons to the evening vespers originates from the scriptural tradition that the Savior comes during the evening of the world—*vergente mundi vespere*. Mary's womb is full and ready to deliver as the season nears completion; dawn arrives and we ardently await the sunrise that heralds the birth, "the tomorrow ripe with Christ."

The 'O' antiphons are distinctive meditations on Advent and the coming of the One for whom we urgently wait. They open with an invocation for the Christ identified with divine titles and prerogatives. After acclaiming Christ's mission, they conclude with supplication for the Savior's coming and appeal for God's activity in our lives. Praying the 'O's, we ready our hearts to welcome Christ's arrival.

(*Note:* The scriptures cited in the margin are the Old Testament verses from which the 'O' antiphons were developed. The prayer for each day is the actual 'O' antiphon. The Symbols P-4 through P-10 illustrate each 'O' antiphon, and they are supported by a calligraphic 'O' that is reminiscent of our flame of longing for Christ.)

December 17: O Wisdom and Daniel and the Three Youths

Early Christian artists drew upon images from the Hebrew scriptures since they were not comfortable with making renditions of Jesus, and the Hebrew scriptures prophesied the coming of Christ. Israel's stories of deliverance from sin and death and of God's merciful wisdom provided hope and consolation to a persecuted church. The story from the prophet Daniel about the three Hebrews in the fiery furnace, celebrated today in the East, is a reminder that God saves the faithful.

Daniel and his three companions, Shadrach, Meshach and Abednego, were pressed into King Nebuchadnezzar's service when the Babylonians captured Jerusalem c. 606 B.C.E. Acting upon a dream image (Daniel 2:31–33), the king erected a huge golden statue with feet of clay and commanded that all should worship it or be thrown into a fiery furnace. Trust in God gave the four believers the courage to refuse the king. They were bound and thrown into a furnace that was seven times hotter than usual. The Hebrew men were joined by an angel and left the furnace unharmed, singing praises to God, while the soldiers who cast them in it were killed by the heat.

Daniel and his companions did not allow the wealth and power of the Babylonians to distract them from fidelity to God. The days of Advent are quickly drawing to their end; we are in the midst of final preparations to celebrate Christmas. Overwhelmed and distracted by too much to do, we begin

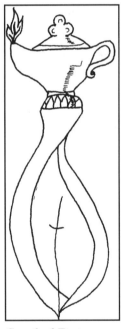

Symbol P-4

I [wisdom] came forth from the mouth of the Most High, and covered the earth like a mist.
—*Sirach 24:3*

She [wisdom] reaches mightily from one end of the earth to the other, and she orders all things well.
—*Wisdom 8:1*

For the LORD gives wisdom; from his mouth come knowledge and understanding.
—*Proverbs 2:6*

59

the 'O' antiphons with an appeal for wisdom. Wisdom comes to teach us to follow Christ with a singleness of heart when we are cast into the furnace of consumerism. We appeal for wisdom from God to become a courageous people, leading the world into justice and peace.

The first antiphon cuts to the essence of who comes to "pitch [her] tent among us" (John 1:14) and to teach us "the way, the truth, and the life" (John 14:6). It is wisdom, *Sophia*, the Word of God, the *logos*, present before creation, that comes in the person of Jesus to unite humanity with God. In short, Christ reveals the wisdom of God.

"Teach us to number our days, that we may gain a heart of wisdom" (Psalm 90:12 NKJV). How is the Advent calendar fostering your desire to follow God with a singleness of heart during the most frenetic season of the year? Is it helping you to focus on God and to see the unity of things? Are you ready to welcome the One who comes to dwell with us?

Antiphon. O Wisdom, you come forth from the mouth of the Most High. You fill the universe and hold all things together in a strong yet gentle manner. O come to teach us the way of truth.

Symbol 49/P-4. The perpetually burning lamp is a symbol of God's eternal wisdom and presence with us, of the Advent of Christ, who brings us enlightenment, knowledge and guidance.

December 18: O Adonai

Symbol P-5

The one who comes is the God revealed to Moses. The divine name disclosed to Moses, I AM WHO I AM (Exodus 3:15) or YHWH, a name too sacred to utter, is substituted with the Hebrew word *Adonai* meaning "Lord." The name signals God's everlasting presence with us. God comes longing to be in personal relationship with humanity, and to that end, God makes a covenant with Moses. *Adonai*, our leader, is the one upon whom all else depends, whose Law teaches us right conduct and the standards by which we are judged: a crime against humanity is a crime against God. *Adonai* is our God, who brings us out of bondage into an enduring relationship and fulfills the promise of peace and freedom.

The etymology of the word "Lord" is "keeper of the bread." In the Gospel of John, Jesus confesses "I am the bread of life" (6:35). The bread came first as the Law, but when we did not ingest it, the God of power and might came simply and humbly, enfleshed as a baby in

There the angel of the LORD [Adonai] appeared to [Moses] in a flame of fire out of a bush; he looked, and the bush was blazing, yet it was not burned up.
—Exodus 3:2

"I will redeem you with an outstretched arm and with mighty acts of judgment. I will take you as my people, and I will be your God."
—Exodus 6:6-7

I am the LORD your God.
—Exodus 20:2

"It is I, announcing vindication, mighty to save."
—Isaiah 63:1

the person of Jesus. *Adonai*, the keeper of the bread, sends bread, the routine sustenance of life, so that we may have life abundantly. The ordinary stuff of life, bread, is the substance of God's extraordinary revelation and presence. Wake up! See God who comes in the everyday to give us life and to sustain us as instruments of God's reign.

Where and how do you see God? Share an occasion when God appeared to you. God's appearance calls us to respond. How can you deepen your response to God this Advent?

Antiphon. O *Adonai* and leader of Israel, you appeared to Moses in a burning bush and you gave him the Law on Sinai. O come and save us with your mighty power.

Symbol 8/P-5. The burning bush is the symbol of God's eternal leadership and revelation. It is also a prototype of the virgin birth since Mary's virginity remained intact, like the bush which was not consumed by fire.

Symbol 50

December 19: O Root of Jesse

In an obscure plant rendered meaningless over time, we place our hope. The third antiphon draws our attention to a seemingly dormant root, resembling a bulb in winter, that holds God's promise. The root of Jesse stands for the nation Israel, whose fulfillment is attained in the birth of Christ. Jesus is the incarnation of the wholeness (holiness) of God, the vine, and we, the branches, are the people of God, grafted back onto the Creator through him (John 15:5).

Jesus shows the way out of darkness into light: love of God and one another, prayer and bearing fruit. It is the way of the suffering servant who is one with God and one with the people—the one who was denied justice yet brings justice to the world.[21] Jesus is identified as the suffering servant through his baptism and ministry, his humiliation and rejection, his death and resurrection. Our call is to live as the servant community, always relying on God's abiding love and justice.

Symbol P-6

Antiphon. O Root of Jesse, you stand as a signal for the nations; kings fall silent before you whom the peoples acclaim. O come to deliver us, and do not delay.

Symbol 50/P-6. Traditionally any plant with a flower (Jesus) and root (Jesse) or a six-pointed star (root) with a chi rho (Jesus) may be used. To remind us that Jesus is the ensign (signal) to the nations and the flower that blooms at the dawn of the darkest night, a rooted poinsettia or Christmas

On that day the root of Jesse shall stand as a signal to the peoples; the nations shall inquire of him, and his dwelling shall be glorious.
—Isaiah 11:10

So he [my servant] shall startle many nations; kings shall shut their mouths because of him.
—Isaiah 52:15

I bring my deliverance, it is not far off, and my salvation will not tarry.
—Isaiah 46:13

I will place on his shoulder the key of the house of David; he shall open, and no one shall shut; he shall shut, and no one shall open.
—Isaiah 22:22,
    cf. Revelation 3:7

To open the eyes that are blind, to bring out the prisoners from the dungeon, from the prison those who sit in darkness.
—Isaiah 42:7

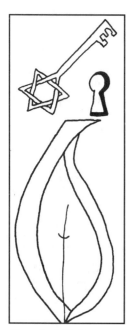

Symbol P-7

rose on a field of ensign blue (the dark gray blue just before dawn) is fitting (see also Symbol 14).

December 20: O Key of David and Esther (c. 470 B.C.E.)

Mercy and judgment are two sides of one coin. On the day of the Lord all creation will be sifted and the wheat will be gleaned from the weeds (Matthew 13:30). While we wait for God's final Advent, God continues to be involved in creation, encouraging and sustaining creatures ensnared by evil.

The book of Esther (c. 150 B.C.E.) tells a tale of persecution and deliverance. Esther was a beautiful Jewish maiden chosen by the Persian king, Ahasuerus, to be his queen. Ahasuerus did not know Esther was a Jew and she did not tell him until the king's chief advisor, Haman, determined to have all Jews killed. Haman was angered by Mordecai, Esther's cousin, who refused to obey Haman's unjust orders. Mordecai insisted that Esther reveal her identity to the king and plea for her people's lives. Esther feared for her own life but agreed. For three nights Esther wooed the king, and when he offered her anything she wanted, she asked for the protection of her people's lives. King Ahasuerus granted her request and hung Haman in their stead. The Jews, saved, celebrated with great feasting. Jews today read and celebrate the story of Esther at their feast of *Purim*.

In an ambiguous story of faithfulness and deceit, of virtue and vice, Esther uses the symbolic key of authority to gain an audience with the king, to request freedom for her people and to demand the condemnation of Haman. We, too, are caught in a world of ambiguity and are ourselves wheat and weeds. The Gospel of John identifies Jesus as "the door of the sheep" (10:7) that reveals what is of God and what is not. By way of death and resurrection, Jesus is our assurance that evil is conquered and that good triumphs over evil, once and for all. The Incarnation opens the gate to heaven and like sheep we are led away from evil through the gate into freedom. This is a good day to decorate the doors of our homes with wreaths of welcome to symbolize the opening of our heart's door to Jesus and the riches of his grace and love.

Antiphon. O key of David and scepter of Israel, what you open no one else can close; and what you close no one can open. O come and lead the captive from prison; free us who sit in darkness and in the shadow of death.

Symbol 51/P-7. A key with the star of David for the hand piece reminds us of the shepherd boy David, who was called to kingship by God. Christ is the master key, the King of kings, who solves the riddle of what is wheat and what is weed.

December 21: O Dayspring and Thomas the Apostle

We long for the dawn of the new age when God will fulfill the promise to bring us out of darkness into the healing light of forgiveness; when the demons of darkness are driven away and all creation is sanctified; when confusion is replaced with enduring joy and understanding; when we witness the coming of Christ and we become twins with the apostle Thomas, whom we honor today.

Thomas, called the Twin, displayed courageous loyalty to Jesus because he recognized him to be the Light of the world; yet his faith began to waver when Jesus talked about his impending death and resurrection. Later, separated from the other apostles, Thomas refused to believe in the resurrection unless he saw and touched Jesus himself.[22] Back in community with the disciples, Thomas was granted visible proof of the resurrection and believed.

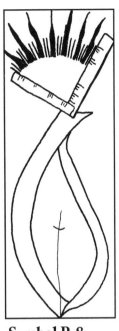

Symbol P-8

Thomas exemplifies the foundations of the church: faith, doubt and community. Faith gives us the courage to persevere in a state of grace through the trials of this world. A healthy doubt maintains our vigilant seeking of Christ so that we, by grace, may resist the charm and illusions of the world. Community is the "visible proof" of Christ that allows us to recognize and exclaim with Thomas, "Our Lord and Our God!" (John 20:28). Through community we are no longer strangers and aliens but citizens and members of the household of God (Ephesians 2:19).

With faith, doubt and community, we progress gradually in our understanding of who Jesus is until that day we recognize with ultimate understanding the fullness of God's loving relationship with humanity. Indeed, when we understand who Jesus is, "the light of the world" (John 8:12), we share life in God.

The Light of the world comes to awaken us from a barren existence into a dawn of new hope for life. Today, on the winter solstice, the darkest and shortest day of the year in the Northern Hemisphere, we focus our longing on the coming Light and lengthening of days. Traditionally, the winter solstice is a day of great feasting: *Yule* in the north and *Saturnalia* in the south. Gather in community to celebrate the coming of the Son of God. Hold a chilly winter chili party. Invite folks to bring chili, condiments, and a coat for the poor. Then, in the tradition of "Thomassing," send guests home with a sprig of holly or mistletoe as a sign of blessing. (Traditional "Thomassing" is a gathering of baking staples for the poor in exchange for the greens.)

But for you who revere my name the sun of righteousness shall rise, with healing in its wings. You shall go out leaping like calves from the stall.
—Malachi 4:2

The people who walked in darkness have seen a great light; those who lived in a land of deep darkness—on them light has shined.
—Isaiah 9:2

For she [wisdom] is a reflection of eternal light, a spotless mirror of the working of God, and an image of his goodness.
—Wisdom 7:26

And I will shake all the nations, so that the treasure of all nations shall come, and I will fill this house with splendor, says the LORD of hosts.
—Haggai 2:7

Out of them [Judah] shall come the cornerstone.
—Zechariah 10:4

See, I am laying in Zion a foundation stone, a tested stone, a precious cornerstone, a sure foundation: "One who trusts will not panic." And I will make justice the line, and righteousness the plummet.
—Isaiah 28:16–17

Yet, O LORD, you are our Father; we are the clay, and you are our potter; we are all the work of your hand.
—Isaiah 64:8

Antiphon. O Rising Sun, you are the splendor of eternal light and the sun of justice. O come and enlighten those who sit in darkness and in the shadow of death.

Symbol 52/P-8. Thomas is symbolized by a carpenter's set square because he was an architect. The sunrise in the valley formed by the carpenter's rule reminds us of who comes, the Light of the world and of the winter solstice.

December 22: O King of Nations

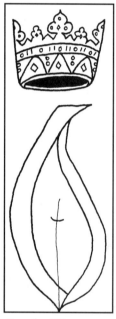

Symbol P-9

Our appeal for God's Advent is coming to a close; the time is short to recognize who comes and to respond with faith. Surely, it is God who comes to shepherd humanity and to fulfill the Old Testament scriptures. We who have watched with expectation and courage are ready to recognize God's voice when Jesus announces: "I am the good shepherd" (see John 10:11–14). Similar to David, a shepherd anointed king, the gentle shepherd is the celestial King of kings. Not a typical king, but a king in complete harmony with God's righteousness, a king who lays down his life freely so that all may live abundantly. All nations long for this king because he reconciles and gathers all people together into one fold. The knowledge and spirituality of every race, culture, and nation will contribute to the full Advent of salvation, the kingdom of God. The Magi (Symbol 30) bearing gifts to the Christ Child symbolize the share all creatures have in the coming of God's reign.

The cornerstone of the household descends from Israel, the house of David, and is the site where the foundation of God and the walls of all people converge. The cornerstone, laid before creation, anchors salvation for those who trust God and will unite all peoples of the world and history into the ideal rule of God. The shepherd who lays down his life for his sheep is a hallowed stone who invites all by name to become living stones of the Temple. Jesus, the King of kings, came humbly in a manger; Jesus, the good shepherd, comes into our hearts daily; Jesus, the cornerstone, will come to reconcile and unite all peoples.

A universal tendency is to honor the sun in the depths of winter because the sun gives life and light. Christians recognize Jesus Christ as the Son of God, giver of true light and abundant life. How do other traditions honor light and the sun? Explore other celebrations during this time of year, or observe a unique family custom and explore its cultural origins. How can these traditions be used to bring people together? How can we be healers and reconcilers in a broken world?

Antiphon. O King whom all the peoples desire, you are the cornerstone which makes all one. O come and save humanity whom you made from clay.

Symbol 53/P-9. The King of kings is king of the heavens and the earth; he is the *Sol Invictus*, the unconquerable Son of God.

December 23: O Emmanuel

Judgment is God's discernment of how we live the days of our lives, and it always includes God's invitation to life. Condemnation occurs when we alienate ourselves from God. God yearns to be with us in a mutual relationship, and God calls us over and over again into a covenant. God is Emmanuel, God-with-us, entirely taking on flesh and living as one of us. God intervenes in history (past), is here with us in community and in liturgy (present), and promises to return as judge (future). No greater judge can be hoped for than a just God who out of knowledge of the flesh determines the merits of our actions. The incarnate Christ wears a crown of humility to judge us.

Jesus is "the resurrection and the life" (see John 11:25–26) because he understands fully what it is to be a limited human being and what it is to be the eternal God. He comes and transforms life from meaningless death to eternal life. The messianic hope of the Hebrew scriptures is fulfilled in the coming of Christ, who in Jesus is God-with-us in an entirely new way. A new Law of love superceded the old Law when God, who understands us, became human and taught us who God is: wisdom, *Adonai*, root of Jesse, key of David, Dayspring, King of kings, Emmanuel. Christ is "the Alpha and the Omega, the first and the last, the beginning and the end" (Revelation 22:13) who is coming soon (Symbols 20 and 57).

In anticipation of Christ's immanent coming, move Mary and Joseph to the crèche and prepare the manger with straw for the arrival.

Antiphon. O Emmanuel, you are our king and judge, the One whom the peoples await and their Savior. O come and save us, Lord, our God.

Symbol 54/P-10. The two candles signify that Christ is the Light of the world: fully God and fully human; the empty manger reminds us to make ready with haste: Christ is coming soon!

December 24–28: Christmas Eve and Christmas Days

Christmas Day and the three days that follow are illustrated for your use during the years when Advent is short. The symbols are labeled with a "C" to identify them as particular to the Christmas season, not Advent.

Therefore the LORD himself will give you a sign. Look, the young woman is with child and shall bear a son, and shall name him Immanuel.
—Isaiah 7:14

For the LORD is our judge, the LORD is our ruler, the LORD is our king; he will save us.
—Isaiah 33:22

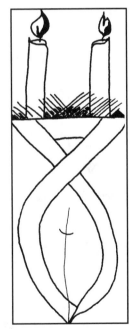

Symbol P-10

December 24: Christmas Eve and Adam and Eve

Today we keep vigil with Mary, Joseph and all creation suffering the labor pains that usher in the arrival of Christ. It is the day of interlude between Advent and Christmas, between expectation and fulfillment, between preparation and celebration. The Christmas celebration emerges from the longing for God-with-us, a longing begun in Genesis when Adam and Eve were exiled from Paradise, where God and humanity walked together. Bells toll in remembrance of the expulsion of Adam and Eve (see Symbol 61), while the people fast in repentance and preparation to welcome the Christ Child.

Adam and Eve remind us that all humanity is from one root. We are all children of God, separated into many branches from the common Tree of Life (Symbol 1). Adam means "humankind" and Eve is Hebrew for "mother of all." Their creation involves relationship with God and one another and is a symbol to us that all humankind is created to love God and one another.

Christmas Eve is the traditional day to bring in the Christmas tree (Symbol 67), to green homes (Symbol 70), to clean house (Symbol 68) and to prepare the lights to welcome Christ. The profusion of light recalls the angelic light that heralded the arrival of the Christ Child to the shepherds who kept watch: the days of darkness are ended and the Light of the world is come. This is the holy night of peace and goodwill, when evil is stilled, while all creation watches with expectation for the birth of Christ.

A traditional evening meal rich with meaning may be enjoyed: fried apples recollect our common humanity with Adam and Eve; abstention from meat respects the animals who were first to see the holy babe; fish recalls the Messiah who comes to slay Leviathan, the scaly beast of evil and death; bread remembers Bethlehem, "the house of bread"; milk and honey emphasize the opening of the gate to the paradise of promise; and an extra place setting signals a welcome to Christ.

Prayer. God, you are the first light cutting through the void.

You are the final light which we shall enjoy forever.

Help us to welcome the light and walk in it always.[23]

"Surely I am coming soon." Amen. Come, Lord Jesus! (Revelation 22:20)

Symbol 55/P-11/56. Adam and Eve look to the Creator's star for salvation (55 and P-11); Santa Claus recognizes the coming of the Morning Star, Emmanuel (56).

December 25: Christmas Day

Today, we gather around the Christmas tree adorned with light and delights to share gifts of love, to read the Christmas story, to place the Christ Child in the manger, to replace the Advent wreath candles with white Christmas candles (or place a white candle in the center of the wreath), to

We know that the whole creation has been groaning in labor pains until now.

—Romans 8:22

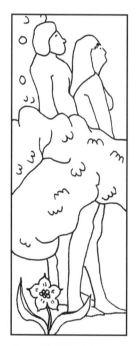

Symbol P-11

Symbol 56

light all the candles and to offer prayers of thanksgiving. God's Advent gives new hope to our lives, and we celebrate Christ's arrival, our love of God and of one another. Christmas is an event to savor for twelve days of gift opening, blazing lights and singing praise.

Three liturgies are celebrated to mark the three ways that Christ comes (future, past and present), and they have a common theme: we share in Christ's divinity because Christ comes to share in our humanity. Let us listen to the message of the liturgies with humility and gratitude for the unimaginable glory of God incarnate.

At midnight, when the earth is cloaked in darkness, a blackness such as in the time before Mosaic Law, Christmas arrives. Awed silence permeates the holy night of God's love made manifest.

At dawn, the Word leaps into the midst of humanity and the darkness gives way to the Light of revelation. The incarnate Word enters the poverty of humanity to live in the everyday, and we are forever changed by it.

At daylight, the Morning Star is born in the hearts of all faithful people. We, like Mary, can only respond, "Here am I." Christ is born in us as we bear the body of Christ in the world.

Prayer. Son of God, you are the light that shines in darkness, eternally begotten of the Creator. You will come again in glory to judge all creation; you have come humbly in the flesh, born of the Virgin Mary for our salvation. We welcome you and ask you to be born in us this day, that through us the world may know your compassion, your peace, and your love. Alleluia! Christ is come!

Symbol C-1. The Christmas Day symbol is the Nativity scene with the seven 'O' antiphon symbols. Can you find them?

To you is born this day in the city of David a Savior, who is the Messiah, the LORD.
—Luke 2:11

Symbol C-1

December 26: Stephen, Deacon and Martyr

The three days immediately following Christmas recognize companions of Christ, whose lives manifest the meaning of Jesus' arrival. The season that begins with a humble birth immediately and honestly faces the cost of discipleship. Beware! The forces of darkness are aroused by the birth and seek to devour the frivolous and complacent.

Today, we remember Stephen, the proto-martyr of Acts 6 and 7. A firm resister of evil through faith, he appeared before the same council that condemned Christ and, like Christ, was the victim of false accusations. Yet he forgave his persecutors. Stephen, which means "wreath," shows us that the way of victory over darkness is faithful service and witness to Christ, regardless of the cost. Place red flowers around your wreath to honor Stephen and all martyrs for the faith. Pray for your enemies and those currently persecuted. Give to the poor or begin a project to help others in need.

For to this you have been called, because Christ also suffered for you, leaving you an example, so that you should follow in his steps.
—1 Peter 2:21

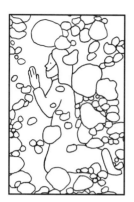

Symbol C-2

Prayer. Merciful and loving God, grant us the vision to recognize the deceit of darkness and the courage of Stephen to stand firmly in our faith during the midst of trouble. By your grace, teach us to love and forgive our enemies and leave all judgment to you. Alleluia! Christ is come!

Symbol C-2. The kneeling figure, surrounded by the stones of death, prays for his executioners.

December 27: John, Apostle and Evangelist

John the apostle, the son of Zebedee, a fisherman, left his family and trade to follow Jesus. He was a faithful friend to Jesus and enjoyed a special relationship with him; he was part of the "inner circle" of disciples: the one who reclined close to Jesus at the Last Supper; the one Jesus gave the care of his mother, Mary, at the cross; the first male disciple to comprehend the resurrection; and the only apostle to escape martyrdom, living into old age.

John the evangelist wrote the Gospel of John, a gospel that uses many layers to present a piercing revelation of who Jesus is, the Son of God. Full of light, it soars to great heights, like an eagle, and carries the reader to the edge of heaven.

And the Word became flesh and lived among us.
—John 1:14

According to tradition, after witnessing with Peter in Jerusalem, John went to Ephesus. One legend tells of how John was challenged in Ephesus to prove the sovereignty of Christ by drinking wine from a poisoned cup without harm. When John made the sign of the cross over the cup, the poison left in the form of a serpent, and he drank the wine unharmed. Thus, on December 27, wine is blessed and toasts are offered to the love of John.

Prayer. Loving God, we thank you for your apostle John, who recognized and followed you faithfully. Reveal to us through his gospel your saving presence, and inspire us through the Holy Sprit to love, follow and serve you in light and truth. Alleluia! Christ is come!

Symbol C-3. John is symbolized by the eagle and/or the chalice with a serpent.

Symbol C-3

December 28: The Holy Innocents

Crimes against the innocent and upright reverberate through the ages and all are affected. Today, we remember the children who died at the hands of Herod and all people who have died and will die senselessly.

King Herod, appointed by the Romans in 40 B.C.E., ruled the Jews in Palestine. A ruthless yet able ruler for thirty-seven years, his obsessive fear of a rival king resulted in the murder and massacre of family, foe and ultimately, innocent children (Matthew 2:1–18). God does not offer a pat answer or justification for the massacre of infants. As we face the reality of evil, we are called to stand, trusting in God's faithfulness and compassion, in solidarity with Christ and all who suffer. The massacre of the innocents emphasizes our dependence upon God's revelation and saving grace.

Traditions abound in remembrance of the mute martyrs who were the first to die for Christ: babies are honored with special celebrations and with decorations on their cribs; liturgies are conducted with children leading the prayers, music and readings; feasting, gift giving and all lights are suspended on this day of mourning.

Prayer. Loving Jesus, let the tears of Rachel express our desolation, let her weep for battered babies and clinical deformity, weep for human cruelty and ignorance and arrogance. Loving Jesus, may we weep with her, may we see what we are doing, what is happening to us; help us repair it soon.[24] Surely, Christ is come!

Symbol C-4. Rachel is weeping for all the innocent victims of crime.

A voice is heard in Ramah, lamentation and bitter weeping. Rachel is weeping for her children; she refuses to be consoled for her children, because they are no more.
—Jeremiah 31:15

Symbol C-4

Chapter 6

Traditional and Personal Symbols and Events during Advent

This chapter contains non-date-specific symbols for common traditions and events pertinent to Advent. They are arranged alphabetically.

Alpha-Nu-Omega

The first and last letters of the Greek alphabet, Alpha and Omega (A and Ω), signify that Jesus, who was in the beginning with God (John 1:3) and will be with us always (Matthew 28:20), is the beginning and end of all things (Revelation 1:8). The middle letter, Nu (N), reminds us that Jesus is with us *now*. The first, middle and last letters of the Greek alphabet form a monogram to symbolize the threefold coming of Jesus

Symbol 57

Christ: in the past Incarnation, into our hearts daily and in glory at the end of time. By teaching us how to live alert to Christ in our daily lives, Advent prepares us for the beginning of the church year and for the end of time

Animals

Animals are honored at Christmas because they witnessed the holy birth and were the first to adore the holy child. St. Francis of Assisi (c. 1182–1226) spoke with and rejoiced over the living creatures of every kind since they, like him, were the work of God's hands. St. Francis' kinship with all creation and his fervent devotion to the humble babe led him to include animals at the living Christmas crèche (see Symbol 69).

Symbol 58

If you have a pet to favor during Advent, do so with the recognition that pets are our kin in Christ and that we all, animals and humans, are called to praise God our common Creator. May our pets remind us of the humility of Christ's birth and our call to live peaceful and kind lives with all of God's creation.

These are written so that you may come to believe that Jesus is the Messiah, the Son of God, and that through believing you may have life in his name.
—John 20:31

Jesus Christ is the same yesterday and today and forever.
—Hebrews 13:8

They all have the same breath, and humans have no advantage over the animals.
—Ecclesiastes 3:19

Baking Christmas Treats

Symbol 59

"I would feed you with the finest of the wheat, and with honey from the rock I would satisfy you."
—Psalm 81:16

Symbol 60

Baking cookies, cakes and pastries at Christmas is a long tradition of grateful charity. From the winter solstice celebrations of the early agricultural communities to the Christmas celebrations during the Middle Ages, baking breads and sweets for others expressed thanksgiving for an abundant harvest and invoked blessings on future crops. Just as God gave the fruit of God's self in the birth of Jesus, so the people gave gifts of their labors with generous and grateful hearts.

Preparing for the Christmas feast, we bake, cook and store an assortment of goodies until Christmas Eve, when they are shared and enjoyed over the ensuing twelve days. As an expression of goodwill and hospitality, treats may be packaged and made available for members of the household to give away to rich or poor, friend or foe, healthy or sick. Sharing gifts from our kitchens with the hungry is a way to remember that feeding the poor feeds Jesus. When you make edible gifts during Advent, plan to give some away randomly.

Bells

O that you would tear open the heavens and come down.
—Isaiah 64:1

Symbol 61

"Sleepers awake!" chime the bells during Advent. Bells summon people to worship and on Christmas they ring out the birth of Christ. Tradition accords to the early fifth-century bishop of Nola, Paulinus, the first use of bells in the Christian church. They were a practical means of time notification, a communal beckoning for all to hear and respond to the call of the church, and a meaningful proclamation of God's creative opening of the heavens to come and dwell with us. In short, the chiming call to worship heralded the presence of Christ and the bid to hear and follow Christ now.

Two traditions are responsible for the use of bells at Christmas. In Ireland, England and Scotland bells tolled with prolonged solemnity at 11:00 P.M. on Christmas Eve to mark the death of Satan, and at midnight they rang out with eager merriment to herald the birth of Christ. Then in 1867, American poet Henry Wadsworth Longfellow popularized the connection with his poem "Christmas Bells."

Listen for the ringing of bells during the Advent season. Where are they rung? What do they signal? Allow them to peal in your heart: "Wake up! Do not let your spirit drowse! Follow Christ, not the world!" What calls your community to follow Christ?

Birthdays

Three persons are remembered on the Christian calendar on the day of their birth: Mary, the mother of God, John the Baptist and Jesus the Christ. All three are Advent people. You who celebrate a birthday during this season are remembered on your Advent calendar. You, too, are an Advent person. You are God's beloved, formed in God's image and called to your particular life. Your birth and life are a gift from God. How do you use your gifts to recognize and honor God? How might you follow Jesus more closely this coming year?

Symbol 62

Before I formed you in the womb I knew you, and before you were born I consecrated you.
—Jeremiah 1:5

Candles

Advent anticipates the coming of Light, which is best symbolized with candles. Candles mark the days of anticipation week by week until the Christ candle is lit to proclaim the holy birth. Candles symbolize the Light of the world, and when two burn, they represent the twofold nature of Jesus: Christ fully human and fully divine. Their flickering lights fluctuate just as our viewpoint of Jesus changes, but at the core, the candle (and Jesus) remains constant.

Candles became particularly associated with Christmas when Martin Luther used candles to decorate a tree at Christmas. Candles during Advent alert us to watch for the coming of Christ. They are flames of hope that shine in anticipation at the eve of the coming promise. In our homes, they brighten the gloomy days of winter by radiating soft light, and they remind us to cultivate welcoming hearts for the Christ Child and all who pass our way. (See Symbols 13, 21–24, 26, 43, 54, 76, and 81.)

Jesus spoke to them, saying, "I am the light of the world. Whoever follows me will never walk in darkness but will have the light of life."
—John 8:12

Candlemas

On February 2, Candlemas celebrates the presentation of Jesus at the temple forty days after his birth. The presentation is rooted in the Jewish Law of purification found in Leviticus 12:2–8. After the birth of a son, the mother was excluded from worship until she made a sacrificial offering to purify herself forty days after the birth. Candlemas commemorates Jesus' entry into the Temple and his meeting with Simeon and Anna (Luke 2:22–38). Just as the rite of purification concludes the period of confinement for the Jewish mother, Candlemas concludes the Christmas cycle. It is named for its emphasis on Christ, the Light of the world, symbolized by candle processions. Its inclusion here is to mark the traditional date that Christmas decorations are taken down and stored.

When the time came for their purification according to the law of Moses, they brought him up to Jerusalem to present him to the Lord.
—Luke 2:22

I am the good shepherd. The good shepherd lays down his life for the sheep.
—John 10:11

Symbol 63

Candy Canes

The cane represents the shepherd's staff, an instrument of protective care. The great prophet Amos was a shepherd whose cosmic vision decried social injustice, called for repentance and pointed to the day of the Lord and its attendant golden age. His vision extends the shepherd's crook into a symbol for the Parousia that beckons "Repent! The Messiah comes quickly!"

The red-and-white-striped candy canes are symbols of Jesus' authority and servant ministry. They remind us that Jesus' love is inseparably fused with the blood of his passion. Christ will come with love and judgment to sift the weeds from the wheat. Life is a mix of good and evil, grace and suffering. Reflect on an occasion of suffering when God's love, like a shepherd's crook, lifted you out of the abyss and into new life. How might you alleviate injustice and offer support to someone in need *now*?

"I am bringing you good news of great joy for all the people."
—Luke 2:10

Symbol 64

Cards

Christmas cards maintain our broad community of family and friends. Providing a means to be in touch with those we cherish, they are personal and concrete gifts of goodwill and affection.

A popular school project, past and present, is a card featuring Christmas greetings and a child's developed skills in drawing and handwriting. This school tradition may be the origin of the Christmas card. The first commercial Christmas card was published in England in the 1840s. Well established by 1870, the custom traveled to the United States in 1875 via German immigrant and Boston lithographer, Louis Prang. Its popularity grew from an original market of about one thousand to a market of mass production in the 1890s. Mass production gave rise to a wide variety of designs, some dedicated to Christmas, some wholly secular.

The choice of cards, their writing and posting require attention. What message do you want to send? Why do you send cards—out of social obligation or friendship? One way to simplify Advent is to choose another, quieter time of year to send cards. Writing cards of hope and love during October and November to send during Advent or writing cards of gratitude and joy after Christmas to send during Epiphany are ways to maintain the seasonal tradition.

As an Advent practice, divide your mailing list into the number of days during Advent and pray daily for a section of your list until all have been prayed for by name. While doing your devotions, also include those from whom you received a card on that day.

Caroling

Hymns honoring the Nativity were evident as early as the fourth century. A hymn of the ancient Greek church, "*Phos Hilaron*," honors Christ the Light. To this day, daily evensong opens with this hymn of praise. It is a candle-lighting hymn that is especially fitting to sing during Advent wreath devotions:

> O gracious Light,
> pure brightness of God eternal in heaven,
> O Jesus Christ, holy and blessed.
> Now as we come to the setting of the sun,
> and our eyes behold the vesper light,
> we sing your praises, O God: Trinity ever blessed.
> You are worthy at all times to be praised by happy voices,
> O Son of God, O Giver of life,
> and to be glorified through all the worlds.

Come into [God's] presence with singing.
—Psalm 100:2

Symbol 65

The Christmas carol evolved from early hymns praising the Nativity and from the ancient custom of singing and dancing in a ring. The term "carol" derives from the Greek and Latin words for the "ring dance." The Greek term, *choraulein*, is a compound of *chorus* (the dance) and *aulein* (to play the flute). The Latin counterpart, *choraula*, fuses *cantare* (to sing) and *rola!* (an expression of joy). *Choraulein* and *choraula* referred to a joyful choral ring dance, usually accompanied by the flute, that was popular with the Greeks and Romans. The custom traveled to Britain via the Romans, and by the thirteenth century, *carole* designated secular dancing and singing.

Medieval minstrels contributed to the development of the Christmas carol during the thirteenth century. St. Francis and his followers traveled the countryside of northern Italy singing joyful ballads about the holy child. "*Adeste Fideles*," attributed to Franciscan Saint Bonaventure (1274), was translated in 1841 by Frederick Oakley into the popular tune "O Come All Ye Faithful!" In Germany, Meister Eckehart (c. 1260–c. 1327) and fellow Dominican mystics promoted vernacular songs to celebrate the birth of Christ. And France produced one of the oldest Christmas carols, "*In Excelsis Gloria!*," written by Thibaud (1201–1253), the French king of Navarre. When the troubadour Franciscans arrived in England in 1224, their melodies were incorporated into the English carole. Gradually, the term carol came to be associated with the song itself: a playful, festive and simple song about Christmas joy.

The first American carol was written by Jean de Brébeuf, S.J., missionary to the Huron Indians, who was martyred by the Iroquois in 1649. The hymn " 'Twas in the Moon of Winter Time" was preserved by the Hurons, who prepared for the Christ Child with fasting and caroling. The singing of carols in public was organized on the streets of Beacon Hill, Boston, in 1885; and in 1909, groups of young people in St. Louis began caroling in front of every house with a lighted candle in its window. The tradition continues throughout the United States.

Christmas carols are songs of joy that comfort the stranger by their familiarity and incorporate individual communities into other communities across time and space. Join in some caroling this Advent. Note when and where the carols originated. Be sure to sing "O Come, O Come, Emmanuel" (Symbols 8, 49–54).

Christmas Tree: Fetch and Decorate

The Christmas tree, symbol of enduring faith and everlasting life, evolved slowly into its prominent role at Christmas. From time immemorial, trees have been sanctified because they connect people with the mysteries of nature and life. Evergreen trees in particular have been long associated with everlasting life. Romans and Egyptians decorated trees to honor their gods. During the *Saturnalia* and the *Kalends* of January, the Romans adorned evergreens in their homes with gifts and decorations of fruits and nuts. The ancient appreciation of trees was imported into the Nativity festival through legend and popular piety. Tradition has it that an eighth-century martyr and bishop from England, Boniface, in an effort to convert the pagans of Germany, replaced their sacred oak with a fir to symbolize a new faith in Christ. An early medieval legend tells that despite the barren cold of winter, all the trees in the forest bloomed and bore fruit at the moment of Christ's birth. Trees blossoming during the dead of winter were cause for reverence, and this legend promoted customs throughout Europe of bringing hawthorn and cherry branches or saplings indoors to force an early bloom in time for the Christmas season. Decorations on the modern Christmas tree evolved from these trees in bloom.

One of the most popular of the medieval miracle plays was performed during Advent. It told the story of creation with a single stage prop: a fir tree decorated with apples. This "Paradise tree" represented the soon-to-be-replaced tree of sin by the coming Tree of Life and Light of the world, Christ. When, in the sixteenth century, the miracle plays were forbidden due to abuses, folks put up the "Paradise tree" on Christmas Eve to honor Adam and Eve. The tree was favored by German Christians, and it is to the Germans that we attribute the Christmas tree we know today. Many stories of its evolution exist: popular in Germany was a wooden pyramid adorned with candles, greens and tinsel to signify the life and light of Christ. By 1521,

Then shall all the trees of the forest sing for joy before the LORD; for he is coming.
—Psalm 96:12–13

Symbol 66

the attendant "Paradise tree" was recognized in the upper Rhine as a living pyramid, and the decorations on the wooden structure were transferred to the living one. Our round ornaments hark back to the fruit on the "Paradise tree."

One German legend ascribes the origins of the Christmas tree to Martin Luther, who was particularly fond of the Nativity gospel. One Christmas Eve, Luther, enchanted with the wonder and beauty of the starry sky, perceived the Christ "who for us and for our salvation came down from heaven." In response to his vision, Luther set a tree up for his children illumined with candles to represent the starry heavens from whence the Christ Child came on the first Christmas.

The evolution and spread of the Christmas tree was slow but sure throughout Europe and America. By the mid-nineteenth century, the tree had become a bounty of adornment and the center of Christmas trimmings. Christians proved resourceful at integrating the ancient reverence of trees, the hope attached to winter blossoms, the medieval "Paradise tree" and the German pyramid to create a tree laden with meaning: Christ, the Light of the world and Tree of Life comes offering freely to all gifts of light and life. What personal memories of faith and life are represented by the ornaments on your tree? What does its bounty symbolize to you?

Two symbols are provided. The plain one is for marking the day to select the tree; the other marks the day for decorating, which is best done on Christmas Eve. If you do bring your tree in early, perhaps the tree could tally the days of Advent: you could place a few ornaments on the tree each day, after prayers are said or good works are accomplished.

Symbol 67

Cleaning House

In preparation for the twelve days of Christmas, tradition advocates a thorough cleaning of the house and a return of all borrowed items. By Christmas Eve, all tools should be laid aside, all unfinished work put away and no new tasks begun that cannot be finished by dusk. "Spring cleaning" at the depths of winter is a way to ready our hearts and homes for the Christmas celebrations. Setting aside a day to thoroughly clean house makes us aware of abundance and encourages charity to help set our sights on the riches of heaven. Helping a child clean out and give away abandoned toys is a useful teaching activity at a time when greed runs rampant. And the gifts received at Christmas will be more welcomed when space is available. Make your housecleaning during Advent sacramental: make it a visible sign of the spiritual housecleaning you are doing in preparation for Christ's coming. Likewise, the arrival of family and guests is a sacramental presence of Christ's arrival. Be ready to offer a clean house and heart at Christ's arrival.

Create in me a clean heart, O God.
—Psalm 51:10

Symbol 68

The Crib

The birth of Christ has been celebrated through visual art since the second century. The catacombs, where early Christians celebrated the Eucharist and buried their dead in underground burial places, were etched with images of biblical salvation, including the babe in a manger. Stemming from Isaiah 1:3 and Habakkuk 3:2 (see Symbol 36), the figures of the ox and the ass were integrated into the scene by the fourth century. But it was not until St. Francis presented a living crèche to the populace of Greccio, Italy, that the Nativity scene became popular. St. Francis believed that if he could see the reenactment of the birth of Christ, his already passionate love for Jesus would be deepened and the faith of the people witnessing the scene would be enriched. On Christmas in 1223, Francis placed a borrowed baby on a bed of hay in a manger flanked by an ox and an ass and preached about the humble birth of the poor king. A solemn mass (Christ-mass) followed on site. This simple act of St. Francis inspired the artists of the Renaissance to create images of the holy family that continue to inspire the faith of Christians worldwide.

In many countries, Advent preparation includes the building, repairing or enlarging of the scene to well over one hundred figures. Assembling the crèche can be a way to embody and bring to life the journey of Advent. December 16, the beginning of the *Las Posadas* novena of Mary and Joseph seeking shelter in Bethlehem (Symbol 48), is a fitting date to set out the Christmas crib. Set up the scene with an empty manger, the animals and shepherds. Place Mary and Joseph some distance from the scene and the Magi yet further away. During the ensuing days, move the holy couple daily until their arrival at the manger on Christmas Eve. The French include a custom of adding hay or straw to the manger as a token of each prayer and good work performed that day. By Christmas, Advent diligence will have made ready a soft bed for Jesus' arrival.

After Christmas services, place the baby in the manger to mark the transition from Advent preparation to Christmas celebration. During the twelve days of Christmas, light candles at the crib and continue to move the Magi until their arrival on the feast of the Epiphany, January 6. This can be a simple practice during the Christmas season flowing from the Advent wreath. Traditionally, the crib remains in place until Candlemas on February 2 (p. 73).

Evergreens

During Advent, evergreens teach about perseverance in the face of hopelessness and about the coming of the One who reigns victorious over darkness and death. Evergreens have a rich and long tradition, pagan and Christian. Peppering a barren and brown landscape are varieties of durable

The ox knows its owner, and the donkey its master's crib.
—Isaiah 1:3

Symbol 69

The glory of Lebanon shall come to you, the cypress, the plane, and the pine, to beautify the place of my sanctuary.
—Isaiah 60:13

plants that flourish and bear fruit. They signal God's never-ending love for us, growth in Christ in the midst of hardship, and the triumph of eternal life over death. Branches in homes are a reminder of Christ's promise to return. They shelter, comfort and refresh the faithful who wait diligently. They beckon the whole person's involvement with their pungent scents, vigorous color, evocation of memories, sticky and prickly texture and herbal flavors. We cannot but help to respond to the gift of the evergreen.

In Spain, the Second Council of Braga (572) prohibited the use of greens at Christmas because it was a pagan practice. Thirty years later, Pope Gregory the Great encouraged Augustine of Canterbury to select popular customs that could have a Christian interpretation. Decking homes and places of worship with evergreens was one such custom. Greening had deep significance for pagan cultures. Ancient peoples used greens to ward off evil, to anticipate the triumph of spring over winter and of life over death, to bring blessings of joy and friendship into the home, and to grant good luck in the coming year. Pope Gregory and Augustine recognized a universal significance of greening and ascribed Christian meaning to the practice. The Christianizing of greening was particularly successful in England and Germany. Decking homes and churches is an expression of joy for Christ's birth and hope for eternal life.

Symbol 70

Greens are a Christmas adornment best hung on Christmas Eve so that they are at their freshest for the Christmas celebration. A myth accompanies this tradition: the wood spirits are invited to make mischief when greens are brought into the house before the Christ Child can govern them. However, some greens are suitable for Advent use, particularly on the wreath. A variety of greens that are available during winter and rich with meaning include the following:

Evergreen trees, such as fir, cedar, cypress and yew, were used during biblical times from the construction of Noah's ark to the Temple. Ancient peoples accorded to evergreen trees the meaning of robust life, since they endured vigorously during winter's demise (see Symbol 66).

Holly symbolizes the burning bush and the virginity of Mary: both remained intact while glowing with the fire of the Holy Spirit. The berries signify drops of Christ's blood on the crown of thorns represented by holly's spiny leaves. Holly used on the Advent wreath symbolizes the unity of Jesus' life from Incarnation to Passion. The berries indicate that the holy child is destined to wear a crown of thorns, and holly's bitter bark foretells the bitter drink on the cross. In Germany, holly symbolized Holle, the pagan mother goddess and patroness of all newborn children. When the pagan candle wheel was transformed into an Advent wreath, the German Lutherans covered it with holly in anticipation of the newborn Christ Child (see Symbol 22).

Laurel is an emblem of victory whose symbolism derives from the ancient Greeks, who crowned their athletic and political victors with a wreath of laurel. For Christians, laurel symbolizes the triumph over sin and death by the birth of Christ and the victory humanity gains through the works of Christ (see Symbol 21).

Mistletoe symbolizes healing and peace. A plant sacred to the Druids of ancient England, it was cut with great ceremony in mid-November. Maidens caught the vine as it was pruned from an oak by a white-robed priest. After a ceremony of sacrifice and merriment, participants returned home with a sprig of mistletoe to hang over their doors for healing and protection during winter's severity. The custom of kissing under the mistletoe probably comes from the Scandinavian pact that if two enemies were to meet under mistletoe, they would lay down their arms and remain at a truce until the following day. When mistletoe is hung over a doorway, it stands for goodwill, peace and friendship. Since mistletoe has medicinal properties, it was a sacred plant among many early European nations and was christened "all-heal." Medieval piety patterned mistletoe into a symbol of Christ, the Tree of Life and desire of nations, who comes to heal all nations; its parasitical growth became an emblem of the Christian life that depends on God for sustenance.

Rosemary, a prolific gray-green herb, is an emblem of fidelity. Its pungent scent is credited for amiable thoughts and sound memory. Its name derives from the same Latin root as *Rorate*, the term used to refer to the winter mass devoted to Mary and the attendant birth of Christ. Both *ros* and *Rorate* pertain to dew and are associated with Isaiah's appeal for the coming of the Messiah, "Drop down dew, ye heavens, from above… and bud forth a Savior" (Isaiah 45:8 RSV). The English recast the term, *rosmarinus*, into a forthright reference to the "rose of Mary," rosemary. Legends flourish about Mary's use of the rosemary bush while on flight to Egypt. One, from Spain, recounts that after Mary spread her violet cloak over a rosemary bush to protect the holy child while he slept under it, the rosemary blossoms were miraculously changed from white to lavender blue. Another story is that Mary lay the holy babe's clothes over the rosemary bush to dry, thereby giving rosemary its savory fragrance. Since rosemary's aromatic leaves and winter blossoms fend off evil, its twig inserted into an apple became a symbol for humanity redeemed through the new Adam. Rosemary complements holly, and the two entwined on the Advent wreath signify the Advent of the One who comes to redeem humanity (see Symbol 22).

Fasting

All we know, we know through our bodies. Through our eyes, ears, nose, tongue and skin, our bodies are instruments for knowing. When we come to know something, we are changed by it. We become new beings with a new perception of the world about us when we integrate knowledge into ourselves via our bodies.

A discipline is something that teaches us by strengthening and correcting our faculties to know. Fasting (usually abstinence from food) is a discipline of the body that can change us when we listen to our body's response to denial. A pang of hunger can be cause for self-indulgence or cause for solidarity with the hungry. Rather than reaching for the nearest morsel of food, we may reach for our deepest yearning: God. Fasting is a discipline that helps us to turn back to God when we move beyond a focus on "what I can't have" to a focus on being filled with anticipation of God's Advent. It is a practice that strengthens our ability to follow Jesus and become his disciples (see Symbols 25 and 34). The trumpet calls us to observe a holy fast in preparation for the Christmas feast and the eternal feast in heaven. If your health permits, select at least one day to fast. Be alert to your body's teaching throughout the fast.

Whoever loves discipline loves knowledge.
—Proverbs 12:1

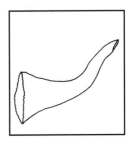

Symbol 71

Fire and the Yule Log

Christmas is the feast of fire and lights because the One who comes, Jesus Christ, is the eternally shining Light of the world. Fire is a consistent symbol for the appearance of God to humanity throughout the scriptures: a flaming sword guards the tree of life (Genesis 3:24); God led the Israelites out of Egypt by a pillar of fire (Exodus 13:21); Jesus comes with fire (Luke 3:16); the Holy Spirit descends on the apostles in tongues of fire (Acts 2:3; see also Symbol 8). John's gospel opens with the testimony that the true Light of life is the Light of the people who shines in the darkness and cannot be overcome by it (John 1:4–5).

Fires were used by ancient cultures for warmth and to drive away winter and encourage the revival of the sun. Vague in origin, the Yule log provided warmth and light for all to gather around and celebrate the return of the sun. The extended Yule festival required a large, long log that would burn continuously to protect the peoples from the evil spirits of darkness. Perhaps from the German *Jol*, meaning "turning wheel," or the Anglo-Saxon *geol*, meaning "feast," Yule celebrated the turning point of the year, when the sun reached its extreme southern arc and embarked on its return journey northward, occasioning hope for spring. Fragments from the Yule log were gathered and stored for protection from fire and lightning during the year and to kindle the following year's fire with blessings unbroken from year to year.

For the LORD will come in fire.
—Isaiah 66:15

Symbol 72

Christianity adopted Yule to the extent that the term now means Christmas and is used as an expression for Christmas joy.

Advent is the time to prepare the hearth for the Christmas fire: to stock the woodpile, sweep the chimney and open the dampers. Do so mindful that fire is ambiguous: it is a symbol for God's presence and enlightenment but also for eternal damnation and destruction. Fire is a refining element that cleanses and purifies. Do your Advent traditions prepare you for the coming of Christ? Refine them until they lead you to recognize the presence of God.

Gifts: Shop, Wrap and Mail

Gifts are a reminder of God's incomparable gift to us: God's only begotten child, the divine gift of love. An Advent focus on God's gift helps to conquer the greed that reigns during the holidays. Keep your eyes on the reign of God and Advent's dawn in your heart.

The Romans offered gifts throughout their winter festivals. During the *Saturnalia*, the wealthy offered gifts to their poor neighbors and the poor gave gifts of greens, candles or incense in return. During the New Year's *Kalends* festival, gifts called *strenae* expressed good wishes for the new year: sweets bestowed wishes for a congenial new year, greens for good health, lamps for a year filled with light and warmth, and money, silver or gold for increased wealth. The Roman custom of gift giving had been transferred to the feast of the Nativity by the twelfth century.

In northern Europe, gifts left anonymously on St. Nicholas Eve recall fourth-century Nicholas, bishop of Myra, who gave money secretly to those in need. Children of some northern European countries receive gifts on December 6 instead of on Christmas Day. The German custom of giving "Christ-bundles" popularized the custom of gift giving at Christmas. The "Christ-bundles" replaced Nicholas' gifts during the Reformation, when Protestants rejected and replaced the Catholic saint with the Christ Child, *das Christkind*, who brought gifts on Christmas Eve. The secretive gifting figure has evolved since the seventeenth century into an American-constructed secular Santa Claus. Whatever your tradition regarding gift giving, remember God's gift that spans gift-giving traditions across the lands.

Shop for and make gifts with a grateful heart and without expectation of reciprocity. Be sure to include a needy person on your list. Following the Magi, prepare to give in the spirit of recognizing Christ in the other. Gift wrapping and mailing are signs of anticipation: that we, an Advent people, are waiting expectantly for God's ultimate gift to us to be revealed at its arrival.

Every generous act of giving, with every perfect gift, is from above, coming down from the Father of lights.
—James 1:17

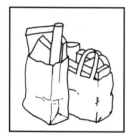

Symbol 73

Symbol 74

Symbol 75

Lights

Originally, candles were used in windows to signal hope for and welcome to the stranger—who may be Jesus—seeking hospitality. During the sixteenth-century English religious persecutions, the Irish placed a candle in their window to summon the itinerant priests for a Christmas visit. The lit candle guided the priest through the unlocked door into the home where the birth of Christ was then celebrated with great joy. If an English soldier should happen into the home, those inside would state that they were waiting with expectant hearts for the arrival of Mary and Joseph. The soldiers, amused by the apparent superstition, left peacefully. The use of candles in the Irish windows developed into the belief that the Christ Child was alone in the dark, seeking hospitality. Their candles, burning with love and devotion, lit his journey into their expectant hearts. Irish immigration brought the tradition to the United States.

The invention of the electric light bulb brought about the replacement of candles on trees and in windows. Beacon Hill in Boston, Massachusetts, saw the first lighted windows in 1908, and by the 1920s, outdoor electric lights had become a popular American herald of Christmas.

May lights in our windows and on our homes radiate the message of expectant welcome and guide the Christ Child into our homes, where we await the One who comes at the darkest hour to light the world.

The true light, which enlightens everyone, was coming into the world.
—John 1:9

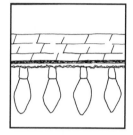

Symbol 76

Lists

Lists help us to make choices, to put a boundary around our wants so that we are not overwhelmed by excess. The Christmas list is a way to focus our desires and help others negotiate materialism's glut.

Children write the traditional Christmas list of desired presents on the eve of the feast of St. Nicholas. Addressed to the baby Jesus, it is placed on the windowsill and taken to heaven by St. Nick when he visits. In South America, children write their lists during the novena before Christmas, December 16-24. They are placed in front of the empty manger for angels to take them to heaven during the night.

Matthew's Gospel opens with a list of Jesus' genealogy, which tells us about who Jesus is. What does your Christmas list tell about who you are? How does your list reflect your true desire? Once written, place your list in your stocking, making it accessible to others to aid their shopping, and then let it go. Be prepared to welcome whatever gifts come your way!

"It is more blessed to give than to receive."
—Acts 20:35

Symbol 77

Olive Tree

Symbol 78

Trees provide shelter and places for rest. The evergreen olive trees provide oil for the menorah, the Jewish stand with seven lamps that represents God's presence in the whole earth. God is our shelter and resting place. The olive branch symbolizes peace, harmony and healing and recalls the branch carried by the dove to Noah, signaling renewal of life. The olive tree's root, stalk and branches are a metaphor for Israel (Jeremiah 11:16), out of which comes the Prince of Peace and healer of nations. Jesus' anguished prayer and arrest took place in Gethsemane, "the garden of olives" (Mark 14:32, Matthew 26:36). Paul broadens the metaphor to include the Gentile Christians, who are a wild branch grafted onto the tree (Romans 11:17).

Olive trees, cultivated since at least 3000 B.C.E., are highly valued in the Middle East for their oil, which is used for anointing and in cooking, soaps and cosmetics. They are harvested during late fall and winter, making them the crop of thanksgiving during Embertide and Hanukkah (Symbols 25 and 26). The wood of the olive tree, excellent for carpentry, recalls Joseph (Symbol 29).

I am like a green olive tree in the house of God. I trust in the steadfast love of God forever.
—Psalm 52:8

Ornaments

Symbol 79

The Christmas tree symbolizes the Tree of Life (Symbol 1), and ornaments can symbolize the life-giving fruits of the Spirit found on the Tree. The virtues on the Tree are identified by Isaiah, the Advent prophet, as the messianic, kingly virtues: wisdom, understanding, counsel, might, knowledge and fear of the Lord (Isaiah 11:2). Likewise, the ornaments on the Tree can symbolize the life-giving death of Jesus on the tree of the cross. We array the tree with ornaments to remind ourselves of the abundant life in the Spirit brought by the Incarnation and by the crucifixion. Jesus Christ, who embodies Isaiah's prophecy, gifts us with the fruits of the Spirit so that we may have life abundantly. Ornaments celebrate God's bounty. (See also Symbol 67.)

On either side of the river, is the tree of life with its twelve kinds of fruit.
—Revelation 22:2

Pageant

The worship of the Christian church from the eleventh through the fifteenth centuries included the dramatization of the life of Christ. Devotion, instruction and participation account for the mystery plays that proclaimed the gospel with song, movement, prayer and word. Abuses out of touch with the gospel story and beyond correction forced the play's eviction from the church during the fourteenth century. Those who acknowledged the wealth

There was no place for them in the inn.
—Luke 2:7

that drama brings to the proclamation of the gospel continued a fruitful tradition of religious drama outside the church. During the nineteenth century, simple devotional plays, particularly about the birth of Christ, were restored within the church walls. In 1851, the children of the German Catholic Church of the Holy Trinity in Boston enacted a Christmas play in the tradition of devotional plays. The play concluded with the children leaving gifts for Jesus in the crib set before the altar. After church, the gifts were distributed to the poor. The occasion met with great success and is broadly imitated today (see also Symbol 48). If you are involved with a pageant, be disciplined about going to rehearsals, having your costume ready and inviting friends to share in the good news.

Symbol 80

Parties

Parties prevail during Advent, though they properly belong to the twelve days of Christmas. Jesus loved a party (his first miracle saved a party, John 2:1–11), and he was criticized for his seeming lack of woe (Matthew 9:14–17, 11:7–19). Repeatedly, Jesus admonishes us to prepare for the heavenly banquet—an eternal party! Jesus comes so that we may have life and have it abundantly. He died so that we may have life eternal. And that life is found in community, in the body of Christ. Allow your focus at parties to be on the folks present. Get to know someone new or someone you have avoided in the past. Rejoice because you are of one body and your presence together makes Christ manifest.

Luminarias (lighted candles in sand-weighted paper bags), used during *Las Posadas* by the Mexican-American communities, provide a path of welcome. They suggest the campfires of the shepherds who kept watch during the night and were the first invited to the celebration of the holy birth.

"The Son of Man has come eating and drinking."
—Luke 7:34

Symbol 81

Poinsettia

Flowers in general abound at Christmas in recognition that Christ's birth is the flowering of the prophets, the flower sprung from the root of Jesse. The poinsettia, a flower resembling the star of Bethlehem, is particularly popular. Its small yellow flowers framed by red bracts are an American symbol of fire and light. The cluster of inner leaves, normally too small to notice on flowers, is unusually large and creates the poinsettia's star-shaped "flower," symbolic of the divine love of Christ. The inversely small flowers are emblematic of his humble birth into the center of life.

Symbol 82

For as the earth brings forth its shoots, and a garden causes what is sown in it to spring up, so the Lord GOD will cause righteousness and praise to spring up before all the nations.
—Isaiah 61:11

The legends of *Flor de la Noche Buena,* "the Flower of the Holy Night," spread from Mexico to North America. One legend tells of a young girl who died of a broken heart on Christmas Eve because she was separated from her lover. Tears of her blood dropped into the Mexican earth and sprouted the poinsettia. In another legend, a young boy's mother died on Christmas Eve and left him without a gift to place in the manger. Desperate, he grabbed a bunch of weeds on his way to church and placed them in the manger for the Christ Child. The congregation laughed at his foolishness, but Christ, deeply moved by the child's offering, bloomed the weeds into a riot of flowers. In 1825, botanist Joel Robert Poinsett from South Carolina traveled to Mexico as the first American diplomat. He admired the unusual flower and brought some cuttings home for his garden. A century later, Paul Ecke of California took over cultivating and commercializing the poinsettia.

Lights are lit outside to guide Christ to our homes. Poinsettias are placed on the porch to guide those seeking Christ to his lodging. Set out some poinsettia plants to alert passers-by that in your home dwells Christ.

Prepare for Guests

Listen! I am standing at the door, knocking; if you hear my voice and open the door, I will come in to you and eat with you, and you with me.
—Revelation 3:20

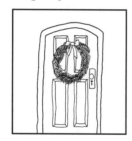

Symbol 83

Symbol 84

"A guest in the home is Christ in the home." The door, a symbol for the prophet Ezekiel, assures us of God's entrance into our midst and of God's continual presence (Ezekiel 44:2). A wreathed door indicates hospitality to all, since all who enter are royalty bearing the presence of Christ here and now.

Planes and trains stand for the extensive travel that occurs during Advent to reunite family and friends. How do you prepare for the return of family members and the welcome of friends? How do you prepare to be a guest in someone's home? Where is your focus? On yourself? Are you trying to impress or improve your status? Is your focus on your guests or hosts? Do you recognize the presence of Christ in them?

Jesus tells us that where two or three are gathered in his name, Christ is present as well (Matthew 18:20). Is Jesus invited? Include someone who may otherwise spend Christmas alone. Note the feelings of hopeful expectation generated while you make the final preparations. Christ is coming soon!

Programs: Church, School, Community

Annually, we attend Christmas programs out of obligation to our children, our work, and our community. Some are religious, but many are not. Feelings of goodwill permeate the air, encouraging friendship. When you attend a public function, how do you respond to the others present? Are some friends and some foes? What makes a foe? Those who are judged in ignorance? Do you stereotype people you don't know? Greet face to face someone you have labeled and observe how it goes. In that person is Christ.

Symbol 85

"And who is my neighbor?"
—Luke 10:29

School Winter Break

Historically, the feast of St. Thomas (December 21) marked the first day of the winter holidays. On that day, students played tricks on their teachers to encourage them to let the children go. A common trick was for the children to arrive at school early and bar the door so that the teacher could not enter. After bantering, the door was opened to a day of fond farewells. How is the last day of school marked in your household? Is it a day of heightened anticipation that incites fun and games? School's out—Christmas is near!

Symbol 86

When they saw that the star had stopped, they were overwhelmed with joy.
—Matthew 2:10

Silence

Advent is the church's winter. A snowflake symbolizes the silent waiting of winter, when all is covered with a blanket of fresh snow. The floral shape accentuates the purity and hope we encounter when we still our minds to listen to the silence that takes us into the presence of God.

A way to practice silence is centering prayer. Centering prayer opens our hearts to God, listens to God's lead and deepens our friendship with Christ. Four stages of centering prayer can be associated with the four named candles of Advent.

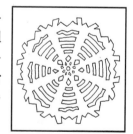

Symbol 87

For God alone my soul waits in silence.
—Psalm 62:1

1. *Watch.* Begin reading a scripture verse carefully and repeatedly. Watch for a word or phrase to jump out; then stay with the word or phrase, repeating it intentionally in a mantra fashion for ten to twenty minutes. Watch for God's lead.

2. *Repent.* When your mind wanders, thank it for the suggested diversion and return to the verse. This is a form of repentance: noticing a wan-

dering from God's lead, acknowledging the wandering without judgment and returning to follow God.

3. *Rejoice* in God's lead to the site of peace and friendship within.
4. *Recognize* God in the silence.

Star

Symbol 88

A star shall come out of Jacob, and a scepter shall rise out of Israel.
—Numbers 24:17

The bright, morning star symbolizes Christ and Christ's messianic kingship. The five-pointed star of Bethlehem stands for the divine guidance that leads to the King of kings. In addition, stars are associated with Mary the mother of God, who is *Stella Matutina,* the Morning Star, and *Stella Maris,* the sea star, who guides Christians through the rough waters of a faithful discipleship. Christ and Mary are two stars whose brightness never fades.

Stars allude to God's abundant mercy because they shine out of the darkness to lighten the way for all. In this symbol, one large star on a field of many stars represents the Messiah who comes for all peoples.

All the material in our universe begins, ends and begins anew in stars! Our bodies are "star stuff," and the Word incarnate is God becoming "star stuff" by taking on a material body. Jesus the Christ is the focal star, the Light of the world, who comes among us and teaches us how to be lights of Christ. An Advent sky on the fabric calendar contains the numerous stars that wait for the One to come; the large quilted star hints at the arrival of Christ.

Tinsel

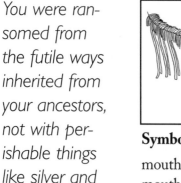

Symbol 89

You were ransomed from the futile ways inherited from your ancestors, not with perishable things like silver and gold, but with the precious blood of Christ.
—I Peter 1:18–19

Tinsel is a metallic material that is used to adorn the Christmas tree with brilliance. Inexpensive, it is often gaudy; however, an interesting legend is attached to the use of tinsel: while en route to Egypt, the holy family, weary from their journey, discovered a cave in which to hide while they rested. Soldiers seeking the family bypassed the cave, confident that it was vacant because a web glittering with the morning dew covered its mouth. Tinsel on the tree reminds us of the spider's web spun across the mouth of the cave to protect the sleeping family. The spider, true to its nature, saved the holy family, and when we are fully ourselves, we manifest God's kingdom. Tinsel hung without thought of God's call to us becomes false show. Are your preparations for Christmas attentive to the One who is coming or are they caught in the false trappings of materialism?

Wedding Anniversary

The Eastern church views the Christian home as an eschatological sign of the coming of God's reign. By their obedience, Joseph and Mary, lovers of God, inaugurated the new age of Christ. They show that a home ruled by the light of Christ (the flames) actualizes the reign of God through love and forgiveness. The central presence of Jesus in a marriage (the cross) sanctifies mutual love and redeems it into a compassionate relationship where hospitality is practiced, the suffering are remembered, and contentment prevails. Celebrate an anniversary that falls during Advent, mindful of Mary and Joseph and of the fact that your love, too, embodies God-with-us. Pray that Christ is the beginning, middle and end of your way together (the entwined rings).

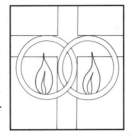

Symbol 90

"Joseph, son of David, do not be afraid to take Mary as your wife."
—Matthew 1:20

Ways to Symbolize Dates Not Covered in This Book

Every household has its own customs, making impossible the provision of symbols for every tradition or event that may occur during Advent. A number of "generic" symbols, the bells or poinsettia for example, are provided for you to assign your own meaning to suit the occasion. Or you may make your own symbol and follow calendar-making directions to add it to your personal calendar. If your unique symbol has a fixed calendar date, make two sizes of the symbol: 1¹⁄₂" and 3". Place the small symbol on the upper right corner of the large date block and the 3" symbol on a felt square (for use during those years when it will be the featured event of the day).

There are varieties of activities, but it is the same God who activates all of them in everyone.
—1 Corinthians 12:6

Chapter 7

Creating Paper-Version and Junk-Mail Calendars for Celebrating Advent

Consider making this version for one or two years before you make the felt or quilted version. The junk-mail calendar will familiarize you with the concept of a liturgically based calendar in a simple way before you have to add the details for making a permanent one.

1. GENERAL INSTRUCTIONS

The color choices are fluid. Focus on the primary colors of Advent, blue with accents of purple and red. Green is acceptable, since it is the color for hope and the greening tradition. Work with the colors you have. If you buy a variety pack of construction paper, use red for the primary color one year and use green the next year. Likewise, use a blue poster board with red for the common dates one year, and use a red poster board with blue for the ordinary squares the next year. Stay flexible, and keep in mind that the color scheme highlights the Sundays, the feasts of Mary and Nicholas, and the 'O' antiphon dates. This is the calendar for using scraps and transforming them into markings of meaningful days during Advent. The sample for this book uses a white instead of purple square on December 20, to highlight Hanukkah.

2. SUPPLIES

Poster board: one sheet of 28"-by-22" lightweight, craft-quality board; blue is ideal, and red, green and purple are suitable

Construction paper (9"-by-12" sheets): two to three sheets of red, two sheets of purple, and one sheet each of pink, light blue and green (the instructions assume a blue poster board)

Paper glue or glue stick

Christmas and/or Advent stickers

Scissors

Pencil

O prosper the work of our hands!
—*Psalm 90:17*

Yardstick
Black felt-tip marker
Old catalogs and magazines and/or the symbols from chapter 10

3. MAKE THE CALENDAR

A. Prepare Poster Board

1. Place the 28"-by-22" poster board horizontally on a large, flat work surface.

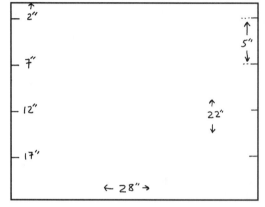

Step 2

2. Using a pencil and yardstick, mark placement lines for the four horizontal rows of date blocks. Working from the top edge down, mark along the left and right edges the following increments: 2", 7", 12", and 17". (On the years that Advent begins on November 27 or 28, make your marks at 4", 8½", 13", and 17½". This will give you room at the top to write an Advent heading.)

3. Lay the yardstick horizontally across the poster board, aligning it along the two 2" pencil marks. Have the yardstick extend ½" beyond the left edge of the poster board (this avoids working with fractional increments). Make a pencil mark ½" in from the left edge, at the 1" mark on the yardstick. Then mark off the columns across the poster board alternating 3" then 1" spaces. On the yardstick (which is ½" off the edge of the poster board) the marks will be at 1", 4", 5", 8", 9", 12", 13", 16", 17", 20", 21", 24", 25", and 28". This will give you seven 3" spaces with 1" spaces between the columns and ½" on both edges. Repeat this entire step for the 7", 12", and 17" marks.

4. Following a current calendar, pencil within the 3" spaces the actual dates, beginning with the First Sunday of Advent and ending with Christmas Eve. Some years, you will have undated spaces at the end. Set poster board aside.

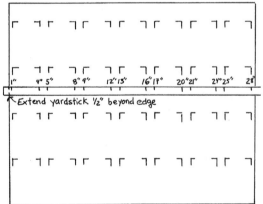

Step 3

B. Prepare Symbol Flaps

1. Cut the construction paper into 3"-by-6" rectangles (from one 9"-by-12" sheet, you can cut six rectangles). You will need nine purple, one pink, two green, one light blue, and nine to fifteen red (depending on the year) rectangles.

2. Fold the rectangles in half to make 3" squares. Glue the squares onto the poster board, lining up the folded edge to the pencil marks. Be careful to

set the colored squares in the right place. First, paste three purple squares in the first column, on the spaces for the first, second and fourth rows. Paste the pink square in the first column, third row. These are your Sundays of Advent. Glue the green squares where you have penciled in December 6 and 24; on December 8, paste the light blue square; and from December 17 to 23, glue on the remaining purple squares. Paste the red squares on the remaining dated spaces. Your base is now ready for the game of finding, cutting and pasting pictures.

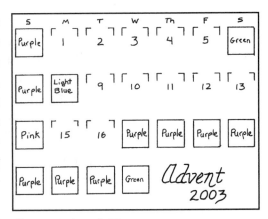

Steps 4, 6 and 13.

3. You will have some conflicts of dates. When December 17 is the Third Sunday of Advent, use pink. When December 6 or 8 falls on a Sunday, use a purple square, and use the square for December 6 (green) or 8 (light blue) on the previous Saturday or following Monday.

C. Complete Calendar

1. Set up the base calendar on a table where it can live for a few days. Gather daily, family and church calendars, and following the directions in chapter 1 on selecting your symbols, write the comments, questions and notices of set dates inside the flaps.

2. Gather catalogs, magazines, scissors and glue. Search through your catalogs and junk mail to find pictures that symbolize the dates you have written in. Let the pictures you find inspire what you write into the open dates. This is a game-like challenge that moves in two directions: finding pictures that represent designated dates and letting pictures you find specify other dates. Use your sense of play. For example, once we found a neat picture of a family chopping and piling wood—we designated a "gather wood and prepare fireplace day." The next year, we did not find a picture about wood chopping but we did find a great picture for Joseph, which stimulated us to designate a day to wonder: "who was Joseph?"

Select 2" to 3" pictures that are readily seen (two smaller pictures are suitable on double dates). As you cut out your symbols, paste them onto the outside flap of the allocated square. You may also select symbols from this book, photocopy and color them, cut them out and glue them onto the outside flap. Combining junk-mail pictures and symbols from the book is another possibility.

3. After all of the squares are covered with pictures, check to be sure that you have written a fitting message or question inside all of the flaps.

4. With a black marker, write the dates in whatever open spaces are left on the outside flap.

5. Write in the days of the week above the columns, and in the largest space available—lower right or on top—write "Advent" and the year.

6. Use stickers with an Advent (preferable) or Christmas theme to tape all of the squares closed.

7. Measure in 1" from the right and left edges and $\frac{1}{2}$" from the top, and mark the intersections with a pencil on both sides. Punch holes where the marks are and use them to hang the calendar.

8. Each day during Advent, open that day's window and follow the message.

Chapter 8

A Felt No-Sew Variation

1. SUPPLIES

Felt: 1 yard of 72"-wide deep blue felt and 9"-by-12" squares—three light purple; two each of light blue and red; and one each of green, white, dark purple, rose pink and gold

Fabric paint: black, purple and red

Stencil letters and numbers: 1" and 1½"

Small stencil brush

1 yard of 200-thread-count white, natural or other light color 100% cotton or a cotton-polyester blend if using transfer method C (chapter 9, section 3, pp. 100-102)

1½ yards of ¾" sew-on Velcro® or 1 yard of Velcro® and twenty-eight small buttons

Velcro® adhesive or E-6000®

1 yard of paper-backed fusible web, ultrahold

Fabric glue: Aleene's Thick Designer Tacky® glue recommended

Old paintbrush for glue application

Pinking and sewing shears, paper scissors

Tailor's chalk

Yardstick

6-8 sheets of photo transfer paper, transfer pen or computer printer paper and coloring supplies (chapter 9, section 3, pp. 100-102)

Iron and board

⅜"-by-36" dowel rod for hanging

All these are activated by one and the same Spirit, who allots to each one individually just as the Spirit chooses.
—I Corinthians 12:11

2. GENERAL INSTRUCTIONS

The approximate finished size is 32"-by-31".

Read the directions all the way through before beginning the project.

You may make this calendar as a simple stitched-felt version. Simply stitch when instructions call for glue, and omit glue and Velcro® adhesive from supply list.

Do not try to sew through fused pieces; the ultrahold web is sufficient.

Letters and numbers may be made using the method outlined in chapter 9, section 4.C; use black, red and purple felt instead of black cotton.

Follow the manufacturer's instructions when using adhesives.

Let adhesives dry between steps. A better bond will be obtained if you put books on the glued pieces while they are drying.

Remember, these are guidelines. Be playfully creative!

3. PREPARE SYMBOLS

Follow the instructions in chapter 1 on choosing your symbols.

Prepare symbols, Advent heading scene and angels (Symbols B-1, B-2 and B-3), following the instructions in chapter 9, sections 3 and 4.

4. CUTTING INSTRUCTIONS

From deep blue felt, cut a 32"-by-33" piece for the background, and cut four 3"-by-32" strips for the pockets.

For the date blocks, cut $3^1/_2$"-by-$4^1/_2$" felt blocks and trim the edges with pinking shears. You will need seventeen light purple, seven light blue, four each of red and white, and two green blocks. Then cut generous 3" felt squares of the following, and trim edges with pinking shears: twenty-five deep blue, three dark purple, five red, and one each of rose pink, light blue, green, and gold squares.

Cut thirty-four 1" pieces of $^3/_4$" sew-on hook and loop fastener (Velcro®), and then cut twenty-eight $^1/_2$" pieces (if using Velcro® instead of buttons).

5. MAKING THE CALENDAR

A. Foundation

1. Lay the 32"-by-33" background piece of felt vertically on a large, flat work surface. Fold over the top edge of felt 2". Glue it in place leaving enough of an opening for a dowel rod to be comfortably inserted for hanging. Turn the felt over so that the sleeve is on backside.

2. Using tailor's chalk and a yardstick, mark placement lines for the four horizontal rows of pockets and days-of-the-week letters. Working from the bottom edge up, mark in the center and along the left and right edges the following incre-

Folded edge

$23^1/_2$"

18"

$12^1/_2$"

$5^1/_2$"

7"

$1^1/_2$"

Steps 2 and 3.

ments: 1¹/₂", 7", 12¹/₂", 18", and 23¹/₂".

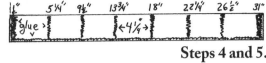

Steps 4 and 5.

3. Line the yardstick horizontally along the parallel marks 1¹/₂" from the bottom edge. Draw a chalk line all the way across the felt background. Repeat this at the other markings until you have five horizontal lines, each 5¹/₂" apart, across the background.

4. On the backside of one 3"-by-32" strip, measure and mark 1" in from each 3" side. Then, from the 1" mark, measure and mark 4¹/₄" increments across the width of the strip ending at the other 1" mark; on the yardstick, working from the left edge, the markings will be at 1", 5¹/₄", 9¹/₂", 13³/₄", 18", 22¹/₄", 26¹/₂", and 31".

5. Paint glue on the strip within the 1" width along the right and left edges; about ³/₈" along the bottom edge, and vertically at the marked increments, to span the 3" height on the strip. Turn the strip over and lay it, glue side down, on the background piece, lining the bottom edge of the strip to the lowest horizontal chalk line. Repeat this procedure with the remaining three strips. You now have four rows containing seven pockets each and one extra horizontal chalk line at the top.

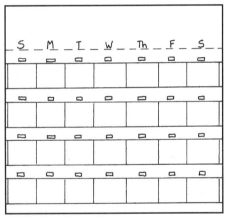

6. Center ¹/₈" above the top edge of each pocket a 1" piece of the hook side of Velcro®. Glue the pieces in place with Velcro® adhesive. (Do not try to use sticky-backed fastener. It will not stick to the felt. If you cannot find Velcro® adhesive or E6000®, epoxy-type adhesives work well. Or stitch the fastener in place with a Z-shaped stitching line.)

Steps 6 and 7.

7. Using the 1" stencils, center a capital "S" above the first (left) column of pockets, aligning the bottom of the "S" to the remaining horizontal chalk line. While holding it in place, paint the "S," using purple fabric paint and a stencil brush. Repeat this step, with the appropriate letters, for the remaining days of the week.

8. Smooth the base section, above the days-of-the-week letters, on an ironing board. Remove the paper from the back of a prepared Advent heading scene (Symbol B-1). Center the scene, right side up, just above the letters. Fuse, following the manufacturer's directions, and careful to avoid touching the painted letters with the iron.

9. Remove the paper backing from the prepared angels (Symbols B-2 and B-3), and place the angels to flank the heading scene, right side up and facing in. Fuse in place.

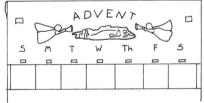

Steps 8–11.

10. Arrange letters with the 1¹/₂" stencils to spell "Advent" above the heading scene. Tape them in place. Using a stencil brush, fill the letters with red fabric paint.

11. Cut four ¹/₂" pieces of Velcro®. Flanking the heading scene, glue the hook sides of two ¹/₂" pieces about 3" down from the top and 2¹/₂" in from

the right and left edges of the felt.

12. With pinking shears, cut four 2" squares from the deep blue felt. Glue the loop sides of four ¹/₂" pieces of Velcro® ¹/₄" from top of each 2" square. Turn the squares over. Using 1" number stencils and red fabric paint, paint the number "19" on one square, "20" on another, "99" on the third, and "0" on the fourth, on the left side of the square. Glue a ¹/₂" hook piece of fastener to the right of the "0" (see diagram in chapter 9, section 6.C-7). (Note: If you are making this calendar after the millennium change, omit the "19" and "99" squares.)

13. Cut a 1¹/₂"-by-15" strip from deep blue felt. Paint the numbers 0 to 9 on the strip with red fabric paint. Leave enough space around each number to cut it out individually. After the paint is dry, cut out each number in generous 1" squares. Cut ten ¹/₂" pieces from the loop side of Velcro®. Glue them to the back side of the number squares (if you are sewing the Velcro®, be sure to sew on the fastener before painting on the numbers). Use these number squares to complete the year on the 2" square with the "0" and hook fastener. (Note: At the change of the decade, you will need to make a new 2" square. Glue the loop side of the fastener on the back of the square, paint a "1" on the left side of the front of it, and glue a hook piece of the fastener to the right of the number. Repeat this step, using the appropriate number, at the change of each decade.) Attach the year squares to the hook fasteners flanking the heading scene.

B. Date Blocks

1. Complete the date blocks following the instructions in chapter 9, section 7. When instructed to sew, glue instead.

2. Substitute the hook sides of the ¹/₂" Velcro® pieces for buttons and the loop sides for buttonholes.

3. Paint numbers using black fabric paint and 1" stencils.

6. FINISHING

Insert a dowel rod through the sleeve at the top of the calendar and hang.

Attach date blocks to the calendar base according to the actual dates of the current Advent season. Place prepared symbol squares in the pockets under the date blocks. On scraps of paper, write a comment, question or suggestion that fits the symbol and place them each in the appropriate pocket.

On each day of Advent, hang the respective symbol square on the date block and use this book to explain the symbol.

Chapter 9

The Fabric Calendar

This version will appeal to quilters and those who enjoy sewing. The instructions are for the making of a quilted calendar with pockets. The directions may appear overwhelming but in actuality are quite simple. All of the cutting and sewing involves straight lines and repetition. Two recommendations: first, make the junk-mail version described in chapter 7, so you better understand the overall concept; second, follow the directions below step by step. You will find, at the end, that you have successfully made a beautiful, life-lasting Advent calendar!

Teach us to count our days that we may gain a wise heart.
—Psalm 90:12

1. Supplies

Yardage is determined from 45"-wide fabric.

Fabric:
$^{7}/_{8}$ yard of dark blue for background*
$^{1}/_{2}$ yard of coordinate blue for pockets
$^{1}/_{8}$ yard of light-medium purple for days-of-the-week background
$^{1}/_{4}$ yard of red for Advent inset
$^{1}/_{4}$ yard of blue for angel foundation
$^{1}/_{4}$ yard of dark blue with stars for sky*
$^{1}/_{4}$ yard of black for numbers and letters
1 yard of 200-thread-count white, natural or other light color 100% cotton or a cotton-polyester blend if using transfer method C (see section 3)
1 yard of backing (a Christmas panel can be used for a banner during Christmas)
$^{3}/_{8}$ yard for binding and hanging tabs (optional)
Batting—34"-by-36"

*Background and sky may be one fabric, equaling $1^{1}/_{8}$ yards.

Felt: 9"-by-12" squares—three each of light purple and dark blue; two each of light blue and red; and one each of green, white, dark purple, rose pink, and gold

Notions:
Twenty-eight assorted small buttons
Two evergreen tree or star buttons
1 yard of $^3/_4$" sew-on Velcro®
1 yard of paper-backed fusible web, ultrahold
Thread, hand and machine needles, pins
Pinking and sewing shears, paper scissors
Tailor's chalk
Yardstick
Safety pins
6–8 sheets of photo transfer paper, transfer pen or computer printer paper and coloring supplies (see section 3)
Iron and board
$^3/_8$"-by-36" dowel rod for hanging

2. GENERAL INSTRUCTIONS

The approximate finished size is 30"-by-32".
Read the directions all the way through before beginning the project.
All seams are $^1/_2$" unless otherwise specified.
All seam allowances are included in pattern pieces.
Stitch length should be 10 to 12 stitches per inch.
Press the seams as you progress.
Do not try to sew through the fused pieces; the ultrahold web is sufficient.

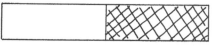 Remember, these are guidelines. Execute with a sense of play!

Right side of fabric. Wrong side of fabric.

3. PREPARE SYMBOLS, LETTERS AND NUMBERS

Symbols, letters and numbers for the calendar are provided in chapter 10.
Symbols from this book may be transferred onto fabric, you may buy symbols on printed fabrics or you may draw your own symbols.
Choose what symbols to use, following the instructions in chapter 1. Don't forget to prepare the $1^1/_2$"-by-4" permanent (P) symbols and the angels and Advent scene for the calendar heading (B symbols).

Cut 1 yard of white cotton into fourteen 5"-by-22" sections for ease in handling. Leave ample space between the images.

To transfer the symbols from this book, follow one of the methods below.

A. Photo Transfer

1. To prevent cutting the book's pages, photocopy the symbols.

2. Once you have chosen the symbols you will be using, color them in with bold colors. Cut them out around their periphery lines and double-stick-tape them onto a plain piece of paper.

3. Take the colored symbols and photo transfer paper[25] to a copy shop that has a good quality color laser copier. Have the shop photocopy the symbols onto your transfer paper with a *mirror* image.

4. At home, preheat your iron to high (dry cotton setting, no steam) for five minutes.[26] Place white cotton on a smooth hard surface (ironing board or table padded with a smoothly folded sheet), and just before transferring the image, iron the fabric to preheat it.

5. Cut the symbols apart, leaving about a $1/4$" border. Transfer one at a time to ensure a good transfer, since a firm, even pressure on the entire image facilitates the transfer.

6. Place the symbol transfer, transfer side down, on the fabric and iron for twenty-five to thirty seconds to transfer the symbol onto the fabric. The key is to use firm pressure while moving the iron around to avoid scorching.

7. While still hot, peel off the paper. Begin at one corner and peel slowly. If the transfer is still on paper, stop peeling, replace the paper and iron ten to twenty seconds more, until the paper comes off clean.

8. Turn the fabric over and press it to set the image. Do not iron the transfer directly; it may stick to your iron. To iron from the topside, cover the transfer with a press cloth.

9. Touch up any poor transfers with your coloring supplies.

Note: You may opt to have the copy store transfer the colored symbols directly onto the fabric for you with their two-stage color transfer process. This will eliminate your need of transfer paper, but it may be a bit pricey. The above method is simple and satisfactory.

B. Computer Scanning

1. Color the symbols with bright, bold colors.

2. Scan the colored symbols with a computer scanner.

3. With the image on the screen, test a print on paper. When you are satisfied with the print, print the symbol onto computer printer fabric.[27]

4. Remove the paper backing.

C. Transfer Pen and Crayons

1. Trace the *mirror* image of the symbols to be transferred onto a smooth, plain pieces of paper with a transfer pen (Sulky makes a good one).

2. Color the transferred symbol with Crayola® fabric crayons available at many fabric and craft stores. (Colors are muted when transferred.)

3. Follow Photo Transfer steps 5 through 10 (above). (*Note*: You *must* use a polyester-cotton blend fabric.)

4. APPLYING FUSIBLE WEB

A. General Instructions

Check the manufacturer's instructions when using fusible web. The essential process is as follows:

1. Preheat iron to medium-high (dry silk setting, no steam).

2. Place a piece of plain paper on the ironing board to protect the board from bleeding colors. Lay the transfer face down on top of the paper. Place a piece of fusible web that is slightly smaller than the printed fabric (to assure that the web is applied to the fabric only) paper side up onto the wrong side of the printed fabric.

3. Glide the iron across the paper side of the fusible web for one to two seconds. Do not over-iron. More heat is not better. Too much heat from the iron breaks down the bond.

4. Allow the transfer to cool. Cut out as directed below.

5. When instructed to do so, remove the paper backing from the web. Place the symbol, right side up, where directed and cover it with press cloth or plain paper. This will protect the transfer and your iron. Some color may bleed. Iron for ten to thirty seconds (check manufacturer's instructions) to fuse. Carefully remove the press cloth. Allow it to cool before checking the bond.

B. Symbols

Apply the fusible web to the wrong side of the transferred symbols *before* cutting them apart. After you have applied the web to the wrong side of the symbol fabric and before you remove the paper backing, cut out the symbols. Cut exactly around the shape of the image, or on those images that are more complex (Symbols 1 and 5, for example), cut on the borderline with pinking shears. Cut out the "P" symbols on the borderline. (*Note*: The symbols to be cut out exactly are great for young children to color since the exact cutting will eliminate any place they may have colored outside the lines.)

C. Letters and Numbers

Before applying the web to the black fabric, use a pencil to trace reversed letters and numbers, provided in chapter 10 (Symbol B-5), onto the paper side of the fusible web. Apply the web to the wrong side of the black fabric. Cut exactly around the letters and numbers. Do not peel off the paper until you are ready to fuse the web to the calendar. Or, you may follow the above transfer method for symbols and cut square shapes around colored and transferred letters and numbers with pinking shears. You will need to prepare the following numbers (the quantity for each is listed in parentheses): 0 (three), 1 (twelve), 2 (ten), 3 (four), 4 (three), 5 (two), 6 (two), 7 (three), 8 (three), and 9 (three).

D. Rectangle F

Cut a piece of fusible web $8^3/_4$"-by-$1^3/_4$" and apply it to the wrong side of one red 9"-by-2" rectangle F (see section 6.C-4).

E. Preprinted fabrics

If you choose to use symbols from preprinted fabrics in your stash, apply the fusible web to the back of the preprinted image and cut exactly around the shapes.

5. CUTTING INSTRUCTIONS

A. Calendar Foundation

A and B: background. Cut four A strips 33"-by-$6^1/_2$" and one B strip 33"-by-$2^1/_2$".

C: pockets. Cut four strips 33"-by-4".

D: days-of-the-week background. Cut one strip 33"-by-$2^1/_2$".

E and F: Advent inset pieces. For E, cut 1 piece 19"-by-$6^1/_2$". For F, cut two 9"-by-2" rectangles.

G: angel foundation. Cut two rectangles, 7"-by-$5^1/_2$".

H: sky above angels. Cut two strips 7"-by-2".

I: sky at side of angels. Cut two strips 2"-by-$6^1/_2$".

J: top sky. Cut one strip 33"-by-4".

K: backing. Cut one piece 36"-by-39".

L: binding strips (optional). Cut four strips 33"-by-$2^1/_2$".

M: hanger tabs. Cut one piece of binding fabric (or sky fabric) 5"-by-25".

B. Date blocks

Cut felt blocks 3½"-by-4½" and trim the edges with pinking shears. You will need to cut seventeen light purple, seven light blue, four each of red and white, and two green blocks.

Cut the following into generous 3" felt squares and trim the edges with pinking shears: twenty-five dark blue, three each of dark purple and red, two each of light blue and gold, and one each of rose pink and green.

Cut thirty-four 1" pieces of ¾" Velcro® sew-on hook and loop fastener.

6. Calendar Foundation

A. Pockets and Background

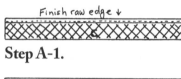

Step A-1.

Step A-2.

Step A-3.

Steps A-4 and A-5.

A-1. Finish one long edge of the four pocket strips C by pressing under ¼", and then press under another ¼" to encase the raw edge; stitch close to the turned edge.

A-2. Pin pocket strip C right side up on the right side of background strip A so that the wrong side of the pocket is to the right side of the background, matching bottom raw edges and sides; baste along both sides and the long raw edge. Repeat for the other three pocket C and background A strips.

A-3. With right sides together, pin the long top raw edge of one background section A-C (the top edge extends above the finished pocket edge) to the long, basted bottom edge of another pocket background section A-C. Stitch, press open, and repeat, adding each remaining pocket background section until all four A-C sections are sewn into one unit.

A-4. Pin one long edge of background strip B to the remaining basted bottom edge of pocket background section A-C, right sides together. Stitch. Press open.

A-5. Pin one long raw edge of the days-of-the-week strip D to the remaining raw edge of the background extension above the pocket, right sides together. Stitch. Press.

B. Calendar Heading

B-1. Prepare the letters (ADVENT), images for inset and angels (Symbols B-1 through B-4, see sections 3 and 4 above).

B-2. Mark ½" with pencil or chalk around the four raw edges of inset E. (These are your seam lines. By marking them, you can be sure that your images will all be within the sewn parameters of the inset.)

B-3. Lay the inset right side up on the ironing board. Remove the paper backing from the letters and inset scene. Center the letters toward the top of the inset to spell ADVENT. They may be arranged in a slight arc or in a straight line. Arrange the scene of Mary and Joseph journeying to Bethlehem below the letters. Hold the letters and scene in place by touching a few edges with the tip of the iron. Once all is in place, fuse following the directions in section 4 above. Set aside.

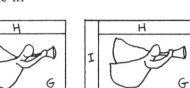

Step B-3.

B-4. Lay the two angel foundation pieces (G) right side up on ironing the board (the pieces are each 7" wide and 5¹⁄₂" tall). Remove the paper backing from the two angels. Center them, right side up, on the foundation pieces and fuse.

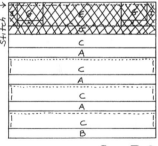

Step B-5.   **Step B-6.**

B-5. Pin the long edge of sky piece H to the top of angel foundation G, right sides together. Stitch. Press open.

B-6. Pin the long edge of sky piece I to the outside edge of the angel foundation (angels face inward), right sides together. Stitch. Press open. (You should have an 8"-by-6¹⁄₂" piece). Repeat steps B-5 and B-6 with the remaining G, H, and I pieces.

Step B-7.

B-7. Pin the inside raw edge of the angel foundation G-H-I to the outside short edge of Advent inset E, right sides together. Stitch. Press open. Repeat for the other side.

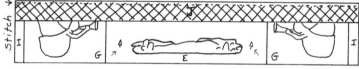

Steps B-8 and B-10.

B-8. Pin the long raw edge of sky top J to the top long edge of the angel inset unit, right sides together. Stitch. Press open.

B-9. Pin the long bottom edge of the top unit to the remaining long raw edge of the days-of-the-week strip D, right sides together. Stitch. Press open.

B-10. Sew the two star or tree buttons onto the Advent inset so that they flank the scene and are placed 2" in from the inset side seams and 2" above the inset bottom seam.

Step B-9.

C. Completing Calendar Foundation

C-1. Lay the calendar foundation on a large table or other large flat surface. Using a yardstick, mark eight vertical stitching lines, beginning at the top seam line of the days-of-the-week strip and ending at the bottom raw edge of the calendar foundation. This will mark quilting lines for stitching strips C into twenty-eight pockets. Work from the center of the calendar foundation and proceed out toward the edges. First, mark the vertical center of the calendar foundation lightly. Then, measure 2¹⁄₈" from the center toward the left edge. With chalk, draw the stitching line. Repeat this, measuring from the center toward the

Step C-1.

		Letter placement				
S	M	T	W	Th	F	S
☑	☑	☑	☑	☑	☑	☑
☑	☑	☑	☑	☑	☑	☑
		Velcro®				
☑	☑	☑	☑	☑	☑	☑
☑	☑	☑	☑	☑	☑	☑

Steps C-2 and C-3.

right edge to create a $4^{1}/_{4}$" space between the two vertical lines that flank the center line. Continue drawing vertical stitching lines, each parallel to and $4^{1}/_{4}$" from the previous line, until the final lines are about $1^{1}/_{2}$" from each raw side edge. When finished, you should have eight parallel lines (disregarding original center line) that designate, within each of the four rows, seven $4^{1}/_{4}$" pockets. Do not stitch yet.

C-2. Lay the calendar foundation on an ironing board right side up, with the days-of-the-week strip D positioned on the ironing board. Remove the paper backing from the days-of-the-week letters. Center the letters between chalk stitching lines and fuse.

C-3. Center the twenty-eight 1" pieces of the hook sides of the Velcro® between the marked stitching lines, placing them $^{1}/_{8}$" above the finished edge of each pocket section. Use a Z-shaped stitching line to stitch them (see the diagram for step C-6).

C-4. Remove the paper backing from the prepared red F piece. Fuse it to the other 9"-by-2" red F piece, wrong sides together. With pinking shears, trim the edges and cut them into three two-sided pinked pieces: two 2" squares and one 5" piece.

C-5. Cut a horizontal buttonhole in which the tree or star button will fit $^{3}/_{8}$" from the top of each 2" square. Remove the paper backings from a prepared number 1 and a 9. Center them below the buttonhole on one square and fuse. Turn the square over. Remove the paper backings from a prepared number 2 and a 0. Center them on the back of the square and fuse. Button onto left button.

C-6. Cut a $^{1}/_{2}$" piece of Velcro®. On the remaining 2" square, place a hook side of the tape on the right side of the square below the buttonhole. Stitch it in place with a Z stitch line. Remove the paper from the back of a number 0. Place the 0 to the left of the Velcro®. Fuse. Turn the square over. Remove the paper backing from two prepared number 9s. Center them on the back of the square and fuse.[28]

C-7. Cut the remaining 5"-by-2" piece into ten 1" squares with pinking shears. Center the loop side of the Velcro® on one of the 1" squares. Stitch it in place with a Z stitch line. Turn the square over. Remove the paper backing from a prepared number 0. Center the number on the plain side of 1" square and fuse. Attach this 0 to 2" square to make the year "00". Repeat this for the remaining nine 1" squares, cutting and stitching nine more $^{1}/_{2}$" pieces from the loop sides of the hook and loop tape and using prepared numbers 1 to 9. (*Note*: At the change of the decade, you will need to make a new 2" square. Put the hook side of a fastener on the right side of both sides of a square. On one side, to the left of the hook tape, fuse a number 1; on the other side, fuse a number 2. These will last twenty years.) Button onto right button.

Step C-5.   **Step C-6.**

Step C-7.   **Step C-7.**

D. A Simple Way to Finish the Calendar

D-1. Trim the calendar foundation edges 1" larger than the finished size, squaring the corners. Trim the calendar backing K to match the size of the assembled calendar foundation.

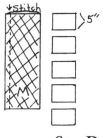

Step D-2.

D-2. Pin the M piece for hanger tabs in half lengthwise, right sides together. Stitch the long edges together. Turn. Press. Cut the piece into five sections, each 5" long.

D-3. Fold each tab section in half crosswise, with the raw edges even. Baste. On the right side of calendar back K, position the five loops evenly across the top edge, with the raw edges of the loops even with the raw edge of back K; place the two outermost loops 1" in from corners. Pin and baste. Safety pin the folded edge of the tabs to back K to hold them out of the way while you finish the calendar foundation.

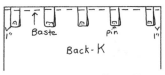

Step D-3.

D-4. To assemble the calendar foundation, batting and backing, lay the batting on a large smooth surface. Center the calendar back over the batting, with its wrong side to the batting. Then lay the calendar foundation on the backing, right sides together. Be sure the calendar foundation's top edge is aligned with the top edge (with hanger tabs) of the backing. Pin all three layers together and stitch ½" from the raw edge of the calendar, pivoting at the corners and leaving an 8" opening to turn. Trim the corners and turn the foundation right side out. Press. Hand stitch the opening shut. Unpin the hanger tabs and move the out of the way so they don't get quilted to the back. Pin the calendar layers to hold in place while quilting.

D-5. Lightly quilt layers and form pockets by stitching over the chalk lines. You may need to loosen the stitch length. Begin at the center lines and work toward the edges; stitch from top to bottom (be careful to keep the tops of the pockets smooth and in place). Quilt the calendar heading by top stitching all four sides of the Advent insert and both angel blocks. You may add more quilting in the top section by echoing the contours of the angels and superimposing a star (see diagram). Congratulations, you're done!

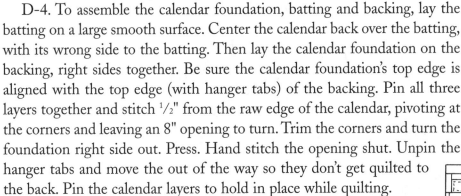

Step D-5.

E. A Note for Quilters

E-1. If you are a quilter, you may choose to finish the calendar using traditional quilting and binding methods. Skip section D and instead:

   a.   Assemble backing, batting and calendar top into "quilt sandwich" and pin.

   b.   Quilt following step D-5 above. Trim to finished size, squaring corners.

   c.   Attach hanging tabs following steps D-2 and D-3 above, but do not pin to back.

    d. Join bias strips L into one continuous strip using ¹/₄" bias seams.

    e. Bind the quilt using your favorite method. Two excellent instructional resources are *Heirloom Machine Quilting* by Harriet Hargrave (C&T Publishing, 1995) and *Your First Quilt Book* by Carol Doak (That Patchwork Place, 1997).

7. DATE BLOCKS

F. Rectangular Base

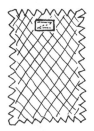

Step F-1.

F-1. Center the loop side of a 1" Velcro® piece ¹/₄" from the top of the back of a 3¹/₂"-by-4¹/₂" felt block (the rectangles are vertical). Stitch in a Z line. Repeat this procedure with the remaining thirty-three 3¹/₂"-by-4¹/₂" felt blocks. (You will have six leftover hook fasteners from Velcro®.)

F-2. Turn the block over and center a button 1³/₄" from the top of the block. Stitch it in place. Repeat this for twenty-eight of the thirty-four felt blocks. Omit buttons on four white and two red blocks.

Step F-2 through F-4.

F-3. Remove the paper from the fusible web on the back of the prepared numbers. Place the numbers in the left upper corner of the colored felts blocks as follows: green—6 and 24; red (with buttons)—21 and 30; light blue—8, 17–20, 22 and 23; light purple—1–5, 7, 9–16 and 27–29. Fuse in place following the directions above. The four white and two red blocks without buttons are for use during the Christmas season. They are not numbered to highlight the movement from Advent anticipation to Christmas celebration.

F-4. Gather the two green, two red (with buttons) and seven light blue felt blocks. Remove the paper from the fusible web on the back of the 1¹/₂"-by-4" permanent symbol for St. Andrew (P-1). Place the symbol, right side up, to the right of the button and just shy of the top of the red felt block numbered 30. Fuse in place. (Remember to use press cloth to avoid ruining the transfer.) Repeat this procedure, placing permanent symbols on the colored blocks as follows (numbers in parentheses are the dates):

Green—P-2, Nicholas (6) and P-11, Adam and Eve (24)

Red—P-1, Andrew (30) and P-8, O Dayspring and Thomas (21)

Light blue—P-3, Immaculate Conception (8); P-4, O Wisdom (17); P-5, O *Adonai* (18); P-6, O Root of Jesse (19); P-7, O Key of David (20); P-9, O King of Nations (22); and P-10, O Emmanuel (23)

Place P-12, Birthdays, and P-13, Wedding Anniversary, on appropriate dates.

(*Note*: Any date could be given a permanent symbol by duplicating the small image flanking each symbol's descriptive text. This is not recommended; it is best to keep the calendar as simple as possible. However, you may have a tradition that should be given a permanent position, and that option is available.)

F-5. Arrange the dated blocks with buttons on the calendar according to the actual dates of the current Advent. If the First Sunday of Advent is November 30, place the red block dated 30 over the first Sunday pocket by hooking it with the Velcro® fastener. Continue until all the dates through December 24 are attached. With this scenario, you would not use the light purple blocks 27 to 29.

F-6. For December 25–30, gather the four white and two red felt blocks without buttons. Remove the paper from the fusible web on the back of the symbol for Christmas Day. Center the symbol, right side up, on a white felt block. Fuse in place. (Remember to use a press cloth.) Repeat this process, placing Christmas season symbols on the felt blocks as follows (numbers in parentheses are the dates): red—C-2, Stephen (26) and C-4, Holy Innocents (28); white—C-1, Christmas Day (25) and C-3, John (27).

On the remaining two white blocks, prepare and fuse any two symbols, such as the Magi (Symbol 30), the shepherds (Symbol 31), or the lion with the lamb (Symbol 35). Use these Christmas season blocks to hang over the appropriate dates when open pockets extend beyond December 24. For example, when Advent begins on November 30, you will use December 25–27; when it begins on December 3, you will need all of the Christmas season blocks. Tuck the length of the block into the calendar pocket to partially conceal the symbol.

G. Movable symbols

G-1. Gather the prepared symbols and 3" pinked felt squares. Remove the paper from the fusible web on the back of the symbols. Center the symbols, right side up, and fuse in place. (Remember to use press cloth to avoid ruining the transfer.)

G-2. Cut a vertical buttonhole through the fused layers that is centered $1/4$" from the top. The symbols are designed with the buttonhole in mind. If a buttonhole falls wrong, adjust it by cutting a horizontal hole or moving it over slightly. Some symbols have designated color squares. They are as follows:

Dark purple—Symbols 21, 22 and 24 for the First, Second and Fourth Sundays of Advent

Rose pink—Symbol 23 for the Third (Rose) Sunday of Advent

Light blue—Symbol 34 for Andrew and Symbol 18 for Mary

Green—Symbol 40 or 41 for Nicholas

Gold—Symbol 26 for Hanukkah and Symbol 52 for O Dayspring and Thomas

Red (Christian martyrs)—Symbols 36 for the Martyrs of El Salvador, Symbol 38 for Barbara, and Symbol 46 for Lucy.

G-3. Cut 3" square slips of paper. On each piece of paper write a thought, something to do or question that fits the symbol to be used. For example, for the First Sunday of Advent, write "Make Advent wreath. What is Advent?" On St. Nicholas' Day, write "Write Christmas lists" and "Who was Nicholas?" For the cleaning house symbol, write "Clean house" or "Finish getting ready for Christmas." Do this for all the symbols (see sample list in chapter 1). Tuck the paper and the symbol into their appropriate pocket for the current Advent. You may also include a small treat for children.

G-4. When dates come into conflict, for example, when December 8, Mary's Day, falls on a Sunday, both dates can be recognized. Hang the second Sunday 3" square over the permanent symbol for Mary. The 3" symbol of Mary is supplemental and may be used in conjunction with the permanent symbol when no other symbol is chosen for that date. This is true for all of the permanent symbol dates.

8. ENJOY

Insert a dowel rod through the hanger tabs at the top of the calendar and hang it.

Each day during Advent, remove the appropriate symbol from its pocket and button it onto the calendar; follow the enclosed message. Use this book to elucidate the symbol and its message.

May your calendar provide you and your household with focus and joy as you observe Advent now and in the years to come.

Chapter 10

Symbols, Letters and Numbers for the Advent Calendar

This chapter contains all of the symbols covered in this book, from specific Advent images (Mary, Advent wreaths, and 'O' antiphons) to reminders of Old Testament and Jewish roots (Adam and Eve, Isaiah, and Hanukkah) to Christmas motifs (shepherds, bells, and the Christmas tree) to household events (a birthday, gift wrapping, house cleaning) to community events (*Las Posadas*, caroling, and school programs). The symbols are designed for you to photocopy, color and use on the 3" date squares of your personal calendar.

The symbols are numbered and arranged in their order of appearance within the book's text. Below is a list of the symbols, their corresponding number and the page(s) on which they are discussed. Those symbols marked with an asterisk have a matching permanent symbol, numbered between P-1 and P-13, for use on the rectangular base of the date blocks. Following the 3" and permanent symbols are four Christmas season images (C-1 through C-4) and the calendar heading images, letters and numbers (B-1 through B-5).

Multitudes, multitudes, in the valley of decision! For the day of the LORD is near in the valley of decision.
—Joel 3:14

Symbols Key and Cross-Reference

Chapter 3
1. Tree of Life–15, **17**, 65, 66, 67, 76, 80, 81, 84,
2. The Dove–15, **18**, 84
3. Rainbow–12, 15, **18**
4. Bread and Wine–15, **18**
5. Seed of Abraham–15, **18**
6. Three Visitors to Abraham and Sarah–15, **18**
7. Jacob's Ladder–15, **18**, 60, 76, 81
8. Burning Bush–15, **19**, 60
9. Freedom–15, **19**, 60
10. The Crown of David–15, **19**
11. Ark of the Covenant–15, **19**
12. Jonah and the Fish–15, **19**
13. Advent Lessons and Carols–15, 17, **19**, 52, 66, 73, 75
14. The Jesse Tree–15, 17, **20**, 47, 62, 84, 85

15. Last Judgment–14, 15, **21**f, 32, 36, 46, 50, 52, 65, 67, 68, 74
16. Daily Visitation–15, **21**, 26, 30, 65, 67
17. Isaiah–6, 19, **23**f, 33, 41, 43, 52, 61, 80, 84
18. Mary–5, 8, 15, 20, 22, **24**f, 30, 34, 35, 36, 37, 41, 51, 54, 57, 59, 61, 65, 66, 68, 73, 80, 88, 89, 109
19. John the Baptist–22, **25**f, 30, 32, 36, 41, 42, 73
20. Alpha and Omega–16, **27**, 65, 71

Chapter 4

21. First Sunday of Advent—Laurel Wreath–2, 5, 8, 15, 16, 19, 26, 29f, **32**, 40, 42, 67, 73, 75, 80, 109
22. Second Sunday of Advent—Rosemary and Holly Wreath–5, 16, 26, 29f, **32**, 73, 79, 80, 109
23. Third Sunday of Advent—Rose Sunday–5, 9, 16, 24, 26, 29f, **33**, 35, 54, 58, 73, 80, 109
24. Fourth Sunday of Advent—Evergreen Wreath–5, 16, 26, 29f, **33**, 66, 73, 109
25. Ember Days–**34**, 81, 84; see also, Fasting, Symbol 71.
26. Hanukkah–5, **35**, 73, 78, 84, 109
27. Angels–6, 24, 34, **36**, 59, 66
28. Elijah—Flaming Wheel–29, **37**, 81
29. Joseph–6, 20, 24, 26, 34, **37**, 57, 65, 66, 84, 89, 93
30. Magi–2, 6, **38**, 57, 64, 78, 82
31. Shepherds–21, 30, 36, **38**, 62, 64, 66, 74, 78, 85

Chapter 5

    November 27: Maximus, Bishop (Use Symbol 21.)–**39**
32. November 28: Kamehameha and Emma, King and Queen of Hawaii–**40**, 44
33. November 29: Dorothy Day–**41**
34. November 30: Andrew the Apostle*–6, 15, **42**, 66, 81, 109
35. December 1: Nahum, Nicholas Ferrar and Rosa Parks—the Lion with the Lamb–17, 21, **43**, 52
36. December 2: Habakkuk, Channing Moore Williams and the Martyrs of El Salvador—the Ass with the Ox–17, 21, 41, **44**, 52, 68, 78, 110
37. December 3: Zephaniah and Francis Xavier–17, 20, **45**, 52
38. December 4: Barbara and John of Damascus–**46**, 76, 78, 110
39. December 5: Clement of Alexandria–11, **48**
40. December 6: Nicholas, Bishop of Myra*—Stockings–5, 8, **49**, 82, 83, 109
41. Nicholas—Anchor with Money Bags–48, **49**, 50, 109
42. December 7: Ambrose, Bishop of Milan–**50**
    December 8: Immaculate Conception of the Virgin Mary (Use Symbol 18.)*–**51**
43. December 9: The Holy Men [and Women] of the Old Testament–17,

Permanent Symbols

Chapter 5: Christmas Symbols

Calendar Base Symbols and Numbers

1.

2.

3.

4.

5. 115

6.

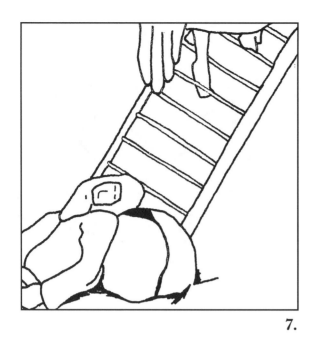

7.

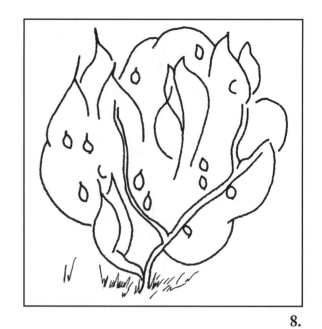

8.

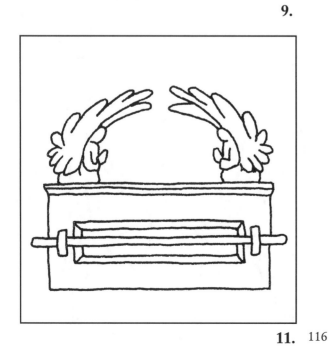

9.

10.

11.

12.

13.

14.

15.

16.

17.

18.

19.

20.

21.

22.

23. 118

24.

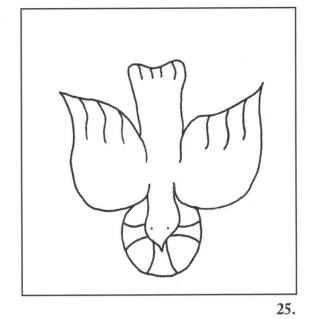

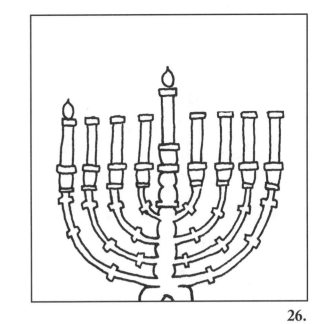

25.

26.

27.

28.

29.

30.

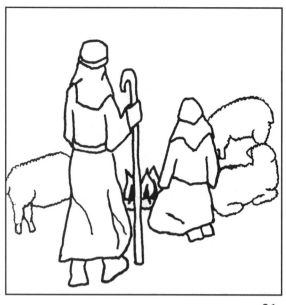

31.

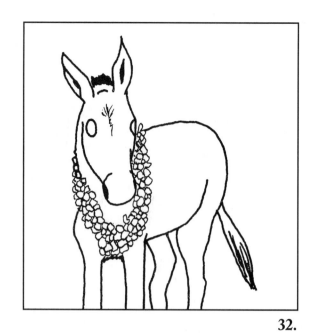

32.

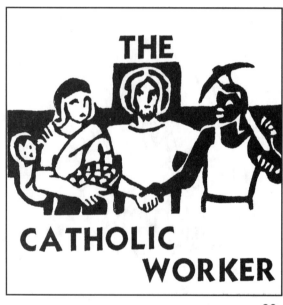

33.

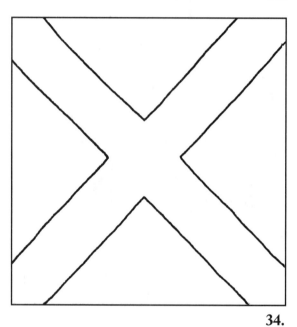

34.

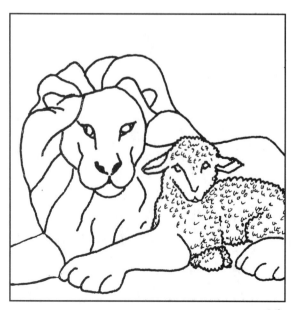

35. 120

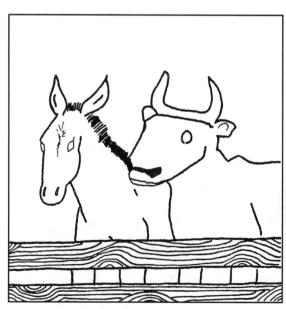

36.

37.

38.

39.

40.

42.

43.

44.

45.

46.

48.

49.

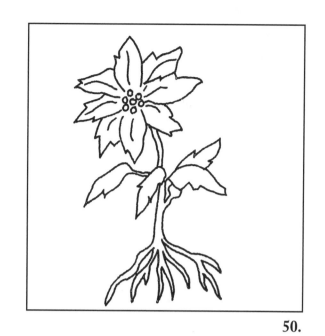

50.

51.

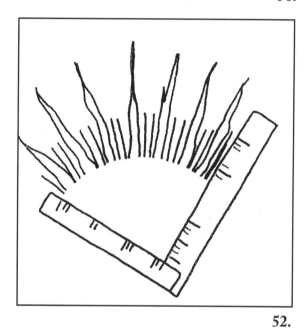

52.

53.

54.

55.

56.

57.

58.

59.

60.

61.

62.

63.

64.

65. 125

66.

67.

68.

69.

70.

71. 126

72.

73.

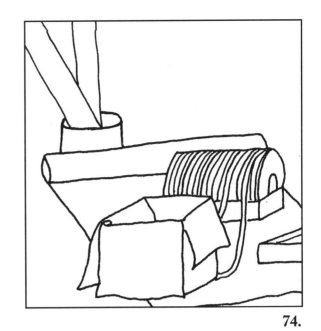

74.

U S Mail

75.

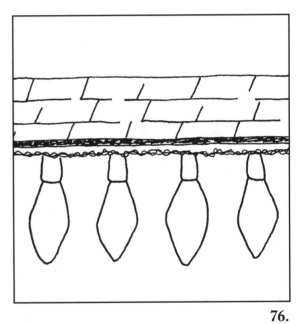

76.

Abraham was the father of Isaac, and Isaac was the father of Jacob, and Jacob was the father of Judah and his brothers, and Judah the father of Perez

77.

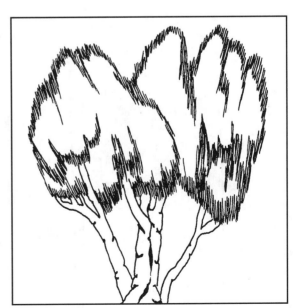

78.

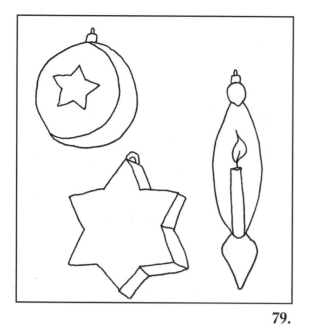

79.

80.

81.

82.

83.

84.

85.

86.

87.

88.

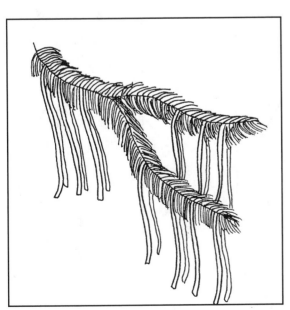

89.

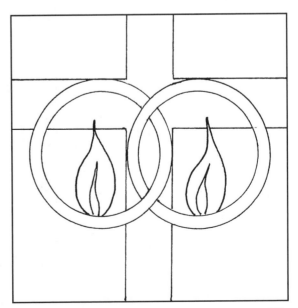

90.

P-1.

P-2.

P-3.

P-4.

P-5.

P-6.

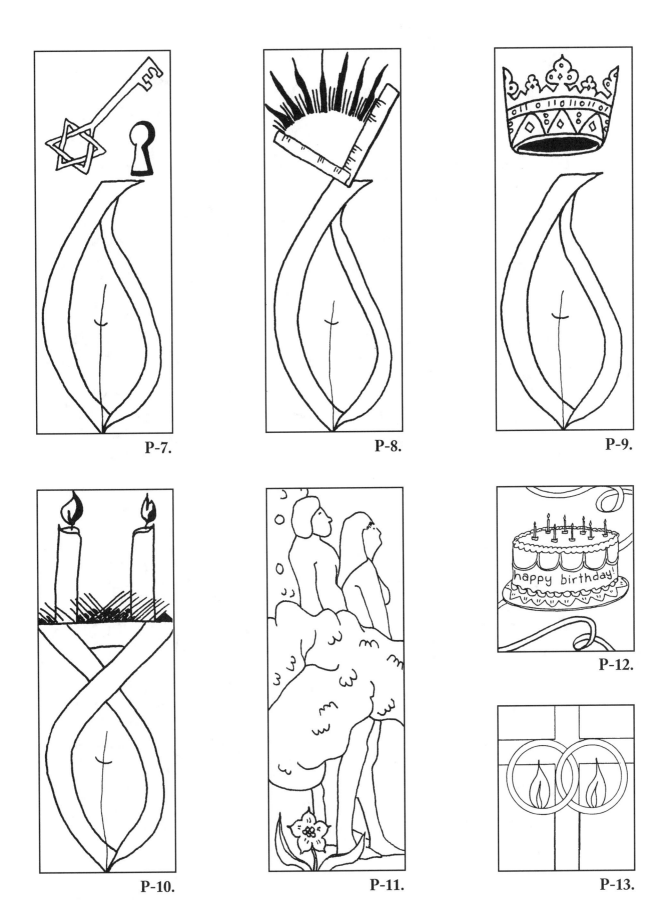

P-7.

P-8.

P-9.

P-10.

P-11.

P-12.

P-13.

C-1.

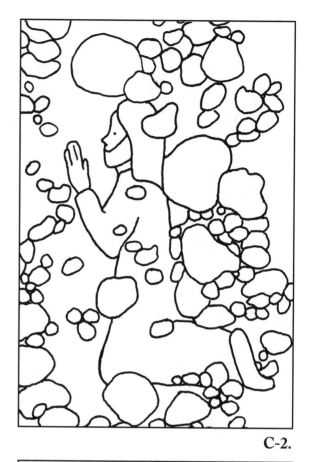

C-2.

C-3.

C-4.

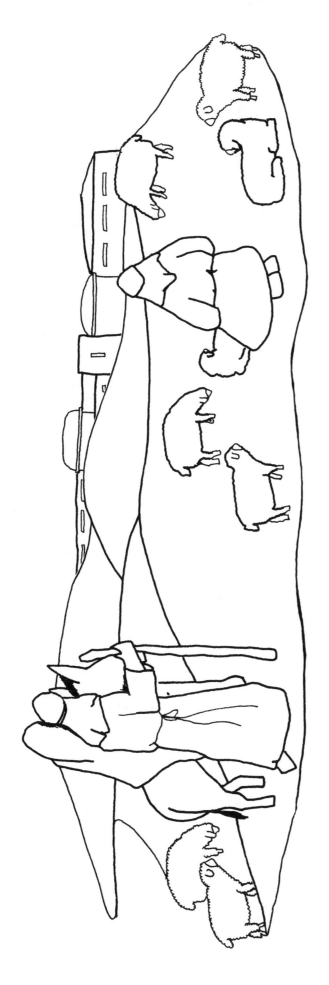

Symbol B-1. Mary and Joseph Approaching Bethlehem

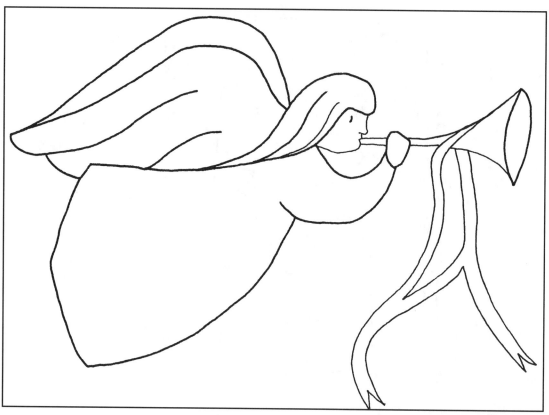

Symbol B-2. Trumpeting Angel

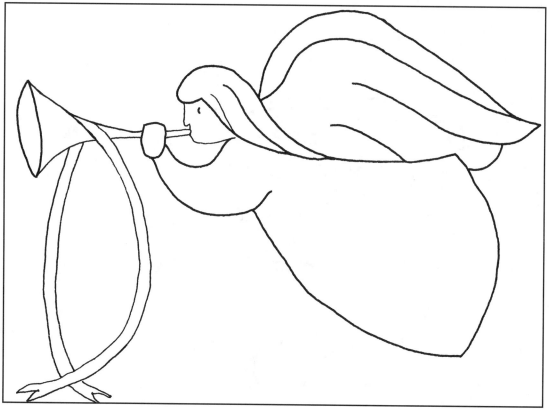

Symbol B-3. Trumpeting Angel (reversed)

ADVENT

SMTWTF

1234567890

Symbol B-4. Letters and Numbers

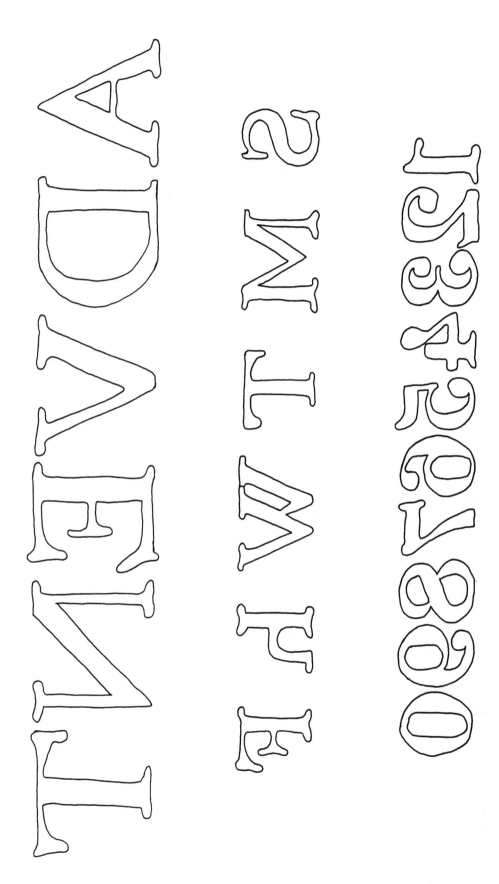

Symbol B-5. Letters and Numbers (reversed)

ENDNOTES

1. Marion J. Hatchett, *Commentary on the American Prayer Book* (New York: The Seabury Press, 1981), p. 39.

2. John Bell, *Bell's New Pantheon* (London: J. Bell, 1790), p. 223.

3. Ibid., p. 83.

4. Francis Xavier Weiser, *Handbook of Christian Feasts and Customs* (New York: Harcourt, Brace & World, Inc., 1952), p. 52.

5. Raymond E. Brown, *a Coming Christ in Advent* (Collegeville: The Liturgical Press, 1988), pp. 16–26.

6. Other references include the "day of God" (2 Peter 3:12) and the "day of Jesus Christ" (1 Corinthians 1:8 and Philippians 1:6, 10).

7. The term *anawim* appears in Numbers 12:3 ("Now the man Moses was very *humble*, more so than anyone else on the face of the earth") and frequently in the Psalms. It refers to the meekest one who lives a humble and God-fearing life.

8. See Deuteronomy 18:15–19, which suggests that the Messiah will be a "prophet like Moses." Moses here is regarded as the prototypical prophet.

9. The four suffering servant songs in Isaiah are found in 42:1–4, 49:1–6, 50:4–9, and 52:13–53:12.

10. This version is from *CSF Office Book* (San Francisco: Community of St. Francis, 1996).

11. *The Magnificat* is based on Hannah's prayer found in 1 Samuel 2:1–10. Rather than being an original song, this song, attributed by Luke to Mary, strings together a series of Old Testament images of messianic longing, God's preference for the poor and the theology of Isaiah's suffering servant. This version is from *CSF Office Book*.

12. The four fasts include the fourth month (June–July), when the Babylonians breached the walls of Jerusalem in 587 B.C.E.; the fifth month (July–August), the mourning of the destruction of the Temple in 586 B.C.E.; the seventh month (September–August), which recalls the assassination of Gediliah in 587 B.C.E.; and the tenth month (December–January), which recalls the siege of Jerusalem begun in 588 B.C.E.

13. Brown, *a Coming Christ in Advent*, p. 33.

14. Thomas Merton, *Disputed Questions* (New York: Harcourt, Brace Jovanovich, 1985), p. 274.

15. The Episcopal Church, *Lesser Feasts and Fasts 1991* (New York: The Church Hymnal Corporation, 1991), p. 413.

16. Isaiah's prophecy, "The ox knows its owner, and the donkey its master's crib" (1:3), is the companion verse; see Symbol 69.

17. Prayer attributed to Ambrose. The Episcopal Church, *Lesser Feasts and Fasts 1991*, p. 90.

18. I am grateful to Raymond E. Brown, who insightfully recognizes the discipleship of Mary in his book *a Coming Christ in Advent*, p. 60.

19. Based on Jacobus de Voragine's reflection on Lucy's life in *The Golden Legend* (Salem, N.H.: Ayer Company, 1969), p. 34.

20. I am indebted to Thomas Merton, who inspired these thoughts in his essay "Light in Darkness," in *Disputed Questions*, pp. 208–217.

21. Daniel Berrigan, *Isaiah* (Minneapolis: Fortress Press, 1996), p. 153.

22. The story of Thomas is found in John: recognition, 11:7–16; wavering faith, 14:1–5; doubt, 20:24–25.

23. Collect for the Third Sunday after Easter, "Christ Our Light," in *A New Zealand Prayer Book*, p. 597.

24. Collect for the Holy Innocents, in *A New Zealand Prayer Book*, p. 678.

25. Photo transfer paper is available at most fabric and craft stores or through craft catalogs. If you cannot find the paper, The Fabric Depot, 866 East Main Street, Santa Paula, CA 93960, will mail order this or any other supplies listed in this book. To reach the Depot, call (888) 868-4988 (toll free) or (805) 525-4556.

26. Check the manufacturer's directions that come with your paper. This book's directions are accurate for most transfer papers, but yours may be slightly different.

27. At this writing, June Tailor makes a 100% cotton computer printer fabric, which is available at fabric and craft stores.

28. If you are making this calendar for the year 2000 or after, omit the placement of the 1 and 9 in step C-5 and the two 9s in step C-6.

BIBLIOGRAPHY

Apostolos-Cappadona, Diane. *Dictionary of Christian Art*. New York: Continuum, 1994.

Auld, William Muir. *Christmas Traditions*. New York: The Macmillan Company, 1931.

Baumgarten, Barbara Dee Bennett. *Visual Art as Theology*. New York: Peter Lang Publishing, 1994.

Beckwith, Roger T. *Calendar and Chronology, Jewish and Christian*. New York: E. J. Brill, 1996.

Bell, John. *Bell's New Pantheon*. London: J. Bell, 1790.

Bernard of Clairvaux, Saint. *St. Bernard's Sermons on the Nativity*. Chulmleigh, Devon: Augustine Publishing Company, 1985.

Berrigan, Daniel. *Isaiah*. Minneapolis: Fortress Press, 1996.

_____. *Steadfastness of the Saints: A Journal of Peace and War in Central and North America*. Maryknoll, N.Y.: Orbis Books, 1985.

Bradshaw, Paul F. *The Search for the Origins of Christian Worship*. New York: Oxford University Press, 1992.

Brewster, H. Pomeroy. *Saints and Festivals of the Christian Church*. New York: Frederick A. Stokes Company, 1904.

Brown, Raymond E. *a Coming Christ in Advent*. Collegeville: The Liturgical Press, 1988.

_____. Fitzmyer, Joseph A. and Roland E. Murphy, eds. *The Jerome Biblical Commentary*. Englewood Cliffs, N.J.: Prentice-Hall, Inc., 1968.

Church of the Province of New Zealand. *A New Zealand Prayer Book*. Auckland: Collins Liturgical Publications, 1989.

Cirlot, J. E. *A Dictionary of Symbols*, 2nd ed. Trans. by Jack Sage. New York: Philosophical Library, 1971.

Cowie, Leonard W., and John Selwyn Gummer. *The Christian Calendar*. Springfield, Mass.: G. and C. Merriam Company, 1974.

Crippen, T. G. *Christmas and Christmas Lore*. London: Blackie and Son, Limited, 1923.

Cross, F. L., ed. *The Oxford Dictionary of the Christian Church*. Revised. New York: Oxford University Press, 1974.

Dawson, William Francis. *Christmas: Its Origins and its Associations*. London: Elliot Stock, 1902.

Day, Dorothy. *The Long Loneliness, an autobiography*. San Francisco: Harper & Row Publishers, 1952.

de Paola, Tomie. *The Lady of Guadalupe*. New York: Holiday House, 1980.

de Voragine, Jacobus. *The Golden Legend*. Trans. by Granger Ryan and Helmut Ripperger. Salem, N.H.: Ayer Company, Inc., 1969.

The tongue of the wise dispenses knowledge.
—Proverbs 15:2

Delaney, John J., ed. *Saints Are Now: Eight Portraits of Modern Sanctity*. New York: Image Books, a division of Doubleday and Company, 1983.

Dix, Dom Gregory. *The Shape of Liturgy*. London: Dacre Press, 1945.

Dunphey, Herbert M., o.f.m.conv. *Christmas Every Christmas*. Milwaukee: The Bruce Publishing Co., 1960.

Episcopal Church, The. *The Book of Common Prayer*. New York: Seabury Press, 1928.

_____. *The Book of Common Prayer*. New York: Seabury Press, 1979.

_____. *Lesser Feasts and Fasts 1991*. New York: The Church Hymnal Corporation, 1991.

Eliot, T.S. *Four Quartets*. In *Collected Poems: 1909–1962*. New York: Harcourt, Brace and World, 1963.

Fast, Jennifer, ed. *La Posada*. Minneapolis: Augsburg Publishing House, 1978.

First Order Sisters of the Society of St. Francis, American Province. *CSF Office Book*. San Francisco: Community of St. Francis, 1996.

Foley, Leonard. *Saint of the Day: Lives and Lessons for Saints and Feasts of the New Missal*. Cincinnati: St. Anthony Messenger Press, 1990.

Hall, James. *Dictionary of Subjects & Symbols in Art*. New York: Harper and Row Publishers, 1974.

Halsberghe, Gaston H. *The Cult of Sol Invictus*. Leiden: E. J. Brill, 1972.

Hargrave, Harriet. *Heirloom Machine Quilting*. Lafayette, Calif.: C&T Publishing, 1995.

Hatchett, Marion J. *Commentary on the American Prayer Book*. New York: Seabury Press, 1981.

Hefele, Right Rev. Charles Joseph. *A History of the Councils of the Church*, Vol. IV. Edinburgh: T.&T. Clark, 1895.

Hoever, Rev. Hugo, S.O. Cist. *Lives of the Saints*. New York: Catholic Book Publishing, 1955.

Hole, Christina. *Christmas and its Customs*. New York: Barrows and Co., Inc., 1958.

Hottes, Alfred Carl. *1001 Christmas Facts and Fancies*. New York: A. T. De La Mare Company, Inc., 1937.

Hynes, Mary Ellen. *Companion to the Calendar*. Chicago: Liturgy Training Publications, 1993.

L'Engle, Madeleine. *The Glorious Impossible*. New York: Simon and Schuster Inc., 1990.

Lefebvre, Dom Gaspar, O.S.B. *Saint Andrew Daily Missal*. Bruges, Belgium: Biblica, 1958.

Maguire, Henry P. *The Icons of Their Bodies: Saints and Their Images in Byzantium*. Princeton: Princeton University Press, 1996.

Marshall, William. *O Come Emmanuel*. Harrisburg: Morehouse Publishing, 1993.

Merton, Thomas. *Disputed Questions*. Reprint, First Harvest/HBJ edition, 1985. Originally published, New York: Farrar, Straus, and Cudahy, c. 1960.

———. *The Seven Storey Mountain*. New York: Harcourt, Brace and Company, 1948.

Metford, J. C. J. *Dictionary of Christian Lore and Legend*. London: Thames and Hudson, Limited, 1983.

Metzger, Bruce M., and Michael D. Coogan, eds. *The Oxford Companion to the Bible*. New York: Oxford University Press, 1993.

Mitchell, Leonel L. *Praying Shapes Believing*. Minneapolis, Minn.: Winston Press, 1985.

Neilson, William Allan, ed. *Webster's New International Dictionary of the English Language*, 2nd ed., unabridged. Springfield, Mass.: G. C. Merriam and Company, 1960.

O'Gorman, Thomas J., ed. *An Advent Sourcebook*. Chicago: Liturgy Training Publications, 1988.

Parks, Rosa, with Jim Haskins. *Rosa Parks: My Story*. New York: Dial Books, 1992.

Patterson, Lillie. *Christmas Feasts and Festivals*. Champaign, Ill.: Garrard Publishing, 1968.

Post, W. Ellwood. *Saints, Signs and Symbols*, 2nd ed. Wilton: Morehouse-Barlow Co., 1974.

Powers, Mala. *Follow the Year: A Family Celebration of Christian Holidays*. San Francisco: Harper and Row, Inc., 1985.

Robertson, John M. *Pagan Christs*, 2nd ed. London: Watts & Co., 1911.

Russ, Jennifer M. *German Festivals and Customs*. London: Oswald Wolff Limited, 1982.

Smith, Homer W. *Man and His Gods*. Boston: Little, Brown and Company, 1953.

Steele, Philip. *Food and Feasts in Ancient Rome*. New York: New Discovery Books, 1994.

Steuart, Dom Benedict. *The Development of Christian Worship*. London: Longman's Green and Company, 1953.

Stevens, Patricia Burning. *Merry Christmas! A History of the Holiday*. New York: Macmillan Publishing Company, Inc., 1979.

Thielicke, Helmut. *The Waiting Father*. San Francisco: Harper & Row Publishers, 1959.

Thompson, Blanche Jennings. *Saints of the Byzantine World*. New York: Farrar, Straus and Cudahy, 1961.

Thurston, Herbert, and Donald Attwater, eds. *Butler's Lives of Saints*. New York: P. J. Kennedy and Sons, 1956.

Vatican II Council. *New ... Saint Joseph Daily Missal*. New York: Catholic Book Publishing Company, 1966.

Weiser, Francis Xavier. *The Christmas Book*. New York: Harcourt, Brace and World, Inc., 1952.

_____. *Handbook of Christian Feasts and Customs*. New York: Harcourt, Brace and World, Inc., 1952.

_____. *The Holyday Book*. New York: Harcourt, Brace and Company, 1956.

White, James F. *A Brief History of Christian Worship*. Nashville: Abingdon Press, 1993.

Zabriskie, George Albert. *Christmas: Its Observance and Ancient Customs*. Private printing, New Jersey: Cliffdale, 1931.

Symbol Key to Quilted Version

Year: 1999

November 28: Symbol 21, 1 First Sunday of Advent—Laurel Wreath
    29: Symbol 72, Fire and the Yule Log
    30: Symbol 85, Programs: Church, School and Community and P-1, Andrew

December 1: Symbol 35, Nahum, Nicholas Ferrar and Rosa Parks
    2: Symbol 36, Habakkuk, Channing Moore Williams and the Martyrs of El Salvador
    3: Symbol 19, John the Baptist
    4: Symbol 26, Hanukkah
    5: Symbol 22, Second Sunday of Advent—Rosemary and Holly Wreath
    6: Symbol 40, Nicholas, Bishop of Myra—Stockings and P-2, Nicholas
    7: Symbol 75, Gifts: Mail
    8: Symbol 18, Mary and P-3, Immaculate Conception of the Virgin Mary
    9: Symbol 17, Isaiah and P-12, Birthday
    10: Symbol 59, Baking Christmas Treats—Dough
    11: Symbol 60, Decorating Cookies
    12: Symbol 23, Third Sunday of Advent—Rose Sunday
    13: Symbol 46, Lucy
    14: Symbol 66, Christmas Tree: Fetch
    15: Symbol 25, Ember Day
    16: Symbol 48, Haggai and *Las Posadas*
    17: Symbol 86, School Winter Break, and found symbol for O Wisdom
    18: Symbol 67, Christmas Tree: Decorate, and found symbol for O *Adonai*
    19: Symbol 24, Fourth Sunday of Advent—Evergreen Wreath, and found symbol for O Root of Jesse
    20: Symbol 29, Joseph, and found symbol for O Key of David
    21: Symbol 30, Magi, and P-8, O Dayspring and Thomas the Apostle
    22: Symbol 53, O King of Nations, and found symbol for O King of Nations
    23: Symbol 68, Cleaning House, and found symbol for O Emmanuel
    24: Symbol 56, Christmas Eve, and P-11, Adam and Eve
    25: Symbol C-1, Christmas Day

SYMBOL KEY TO FELT VERSION

Shown Ten Days into Advent

Year: 2000

December 3: Symbol 21, First Sunday in Advent—Laurel Wreath
          4: Symbol 38, Barbara and John of Damascus
          5: Symbol 64, Cards
          6: Symbol 41, Nicholas, Bishop of Myra—Anchor with Money Bags and P-2, Nicholas, Bishop of Myra
          7: Symbol 42, Ambrose, Bishop of Milan
          8: Symbol 18, Mary and P-3, Immaculate Conception of the Virgin Mary
          9: Symbol 58, Animals
         10: Symbol 22, Second Sunday of Advent—Rosemary and Holly Wreath
         11: Symbol 19, John the Baptist
         12: Symbol 45, Our Lady of Guadalupe
         13:
         14:
         15:
         16:
         17: Symbol P-4, O Wisdom
         18: Symbol P-5, O *Adonai*
         19: Symbol P-6, O Root of Jesse
         20: Symbol P-7, O Key of David
         21: Symbol P-8, O Dayspring and Thomas the Apostle
         22: Symbol P-9, O King of Nations
         23: Symbol P-10, O Emmanuel
         24: Symbol P-11, Adam and Eve
         25: Symbol C-1, Christmas Day (tucked in pocket)
         26: Symbol C-2, Stephen, Deacon and Martyr (tucked)
         27: Symbol C-3, John, Apostle and Evangelist (tucked)
         28: Symbol C-4, The Holy Innocents (tucked)
         29: Symbol 15, Last Judgment
         30: Symbol 20, Alpha and Omega

'Twas the Month Before Christmas

A Coloring and Family Activity Book

by Martha H. King

This coloring and activity book helps children ages 3–10 learn about and celebrate Advent and Christmas. An excellent tool for parents or for church school teachers, the book is filled with craft ideas, puzzles, and word games. All of these activities are woven into a story of two children celebrating the season with their family.

This well-balanced approach to the Advent and Christmas season helps children follow the biblical story that is the focus of Christmas, while it helps them place gift-giving, making cookies, and other activities into context. Parents and children can enjoy a variety of craft activities outlined in the book, such as the construction of Advent wreaths and simple Advent calendars, Christmas tree ornaments, and more. Permission to photocopy individual pages for use during worship services or church school is included.

MOREHOUSE PUBLISHING

Available from

bookstores everywhere

and on the Internet at

www.morehousepublishing.com

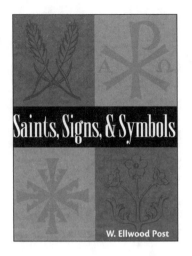

Saints, Signs, & Symbols

by W. Ellwood Post

Through the centuries, the Church has used symbols to represent God, saints, concepts, and important events. This comprehensive collection of illustrations identifies and explains a variety of emblems according to fact or legend, offering the information needed to fully understand their meanings.

This practical reference, valuable to all who work with or have an interest in the symbols of the Church, contains an assortment of categories, including:

- God
- The Four Evangelists
- The Twelve Apostles
- The Holy Trinity
- Sacred Monograms
- St. Mary the Virgin
- Saints
- Crosses
- Stars
- and more

Available from

bookstores everywhere

and on the Internet at

www.morehousepublishing.com

MOREHOUSE PUBLISHING

The New Banner Book

by Betty Wolfe

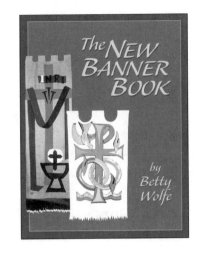

This new edition of Betty Wolfe's classic manual covers all the essential steps and information needed for quick-and-easy church banner construction, including 49 patterns, complete instructions, and tips for designing your own patterns.

Regardless of their skill level, readers can learn how and where to place words and use symbols, choose colors, and make basic arrangements. The book includes idea starters, helpful design solutions, and easy reference sections on appliqués, stitchery and gluing, fabrics, tassels, tabs, bells, finishings, and mountings. It also lists information on tools and materials, and how to enlarge or adapt patterns.

Patterns for seasons, special events, and regular use can keep the church freshly decorated all year round.

MOREHOUSE PUBLISHING

Available from

bookstores everywhere

and on the Internet at

www.morehousepublishing.com

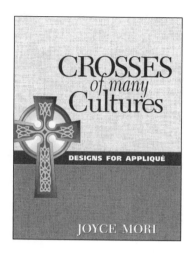

Crosses of Many Cultures
Designs for Appliqué
by Joyce Mori

Throughout the ages many cultures have developed their own designs to depict the cross. A symbol of both suffering and victory, the cross can be used to create a powerful, meaningful image on functional and decorative pieces in the church, home, and office. In this unique collection, Joyce Mori provides historical background along with easy-to-understand instruction and line drawings for twenty international cross designs for appliqué.

Writing for the beginner and intermediate levels, Mori explains several appliqué techniques, from hand and machine sewing methods to no-sewing techniques. The versatility of these designs is evident in the wide array of suggested projects, which include quilts, banners, church linens and vestments, table runners, place mats, apron fronts, and door toppers.

Available from

bookstores everywhere

and on the Internet at

www.morehousepublishing.com

MOREHOUSE PUBLISHING

Sewing Church Linens
Revised Edition
by Elizabeth Morgan

The classic book on sewing linens for the church is back in a revised edition. This complete reference work explains the materials and equipment needed, a variety of hemming options, special instructions on the small linens such as purificators and palls, working with fair linens, white work embroidery, and caring for church linens.

New to this edition are directions for rolled hems, chalice veils, more specific directions, and an improved worksheet for planning shrinkage, special advice specifically for beginners, an updated "Sources and Resources" section, and new patterns.

MOREHOUSE PUBLISHING

Available from

bookstores everywhere

and on the Internet at

www.morehousepublishing.com